THE JEW NAMED JESUS

Other Books by Rebekah Simon-Peter:

Green Church: Reduce, Reuse, Recycle, Rejoice!

Green Church: Reduce, Reuse, Recycle, Rejoice! Leader Guide,
with Pamela Dilmore

7 Simple Steps to Green Your Church

THE JEW
NAMED
JESUS

Discover the Man and His Message

Rebekah Simon-Peter

To Janet –
Blessings on your spiritual
journey!
R S

Abingdon Press
Nashville

THE JEW NAMED JESUS
DISCOVER THE MAN AND HIS MESSAGE

To my grandmother,

Miriam Harris Goldberg,

who inspired in me the love of Judaism

CONTENTS

ACKNOWLEDGMENTS

A book is best written in community. Thanks to both my Jewish and Christian communities who have contributed to my thinking, nurtured my spiritual growth, and engaged me in dialogue. Thanks, too, to the Jewish and Christian scholars whose work has confirmed my questions and sustained me in the search for answers. My ongoing appreciation to Jeanette Baust for great questions. Most of all, I am grateful to my Catholic husband Jerry Gonzales, whose love, support and willingness to see life through Jewish eyes has made life a joy.

INTRODUCTION

The Jew Named Jesus

Discover the Man and His Message

We have come a long way in Jewish-Christian relations. Thanks to the work of the Roman Catholic Church during Vatican II in the 1960s as well as interfaith dialogues that have taken root in communities large and small since then, anti-Semitism and anti-Judaism have greatly declined in American churches.

Unfortunately, these advances in understanding haven't lapped up on every shore nor are they reflected in every Sunday sermon or Good Friday service. There are still vestiges of anti-Judaism in church services today. Stereotypical portrayals of Pharisees abound as do skewed understandings of Jewish life in Jesus' time. Even what we say about Paul and his relationship to the Law needs updating as do the theologies that arise from these misunderstandings. Still, our progress is worthy of celebration.

It's time now to say it loud and proud: Jesus was a Jew. He was born a Jew, raised a Jew, lived a Jew, died a Jew, and was even resurrected a Jew. He was no backsliding Jew or a Jew in name only. He was Jewish through and through. In naming him this way, there is a great message of hope and unity for a divided world in the Christian community, between Jews and Christians, and maybe even in the larger religious landscape.

Recovering this message of unity will require seeing the Gospels and the entire New Testament in a whole new light. Empowering you to try on this new set of lenses—which I call "reading the Bible with Jewish eyes"—is what I set out to do in this book so that we can discover anew the man and his message.

In Chapter 1, *What's a Nice Jewish Girl Like Me Doing in a Place Like This?* I share my own story of how I personally came to this perspective of Jesus. In Chapter 2, *Was Jesus a Christian?* I discuss the biblical evidence that points to an unmistakably Jewish Jesus. At the same time, I'll explore Jesus' relationship to Christianity. In Chapter 3, *Did the Jews Reject Jesus?* I look at Jesus' earliest followers and the religious nature of the early church. In Chapter 4, *Did the Jews Kill Jesus?* I raise the nagging question that has prompted so much pain and suffering in the world—who killed Jesus and why? In Chapter 5, *Has God Rejected the Jews?* I look at the biblical relationship between Jews and Christians. In Chapter 6, *A New Heaven and a New Earth*, I look at the message of unity contained in Jesus' life and teaching that brings hope to a divided world.

My hope in writing this book is that new generations of Christians and Jews will work together for a kingdom of God that is truly inclusive—based in love of God and love of neighbor—without losing the essential distinctions of their respective spiritual traditions. At the same time, I hold out for a stronger acceptance of spiritual hybrids who, like me, who have a foot in both worlds. My vision is a vision of hope that is as old as the Bible and as new as the fragmented world we live in. May it be so! Amen.

1. What's a Nice Jewish Girl Like Me Doing in a Place Like This?

Who Do You Say That I Am?

"Who do you say that I am?" This is the question Jesus posed to his long-ago disciples. In a sudden display of clarity, Simon Peter answered, "You are the Messiah, the Son of the living God."[1] That answer, in addition to being a turning point in the Gospel of Matthew, is also the single greatest point of belief that separates traditional Jewish theology from traditional Christian theology. Christians believe Jesus is the Messiah or Christ, and that he is divine. Jews see Jesus as a prophet at best, a failed messiah at worst, and certainly not divine in any way. Those are two very different perspectives!

I can relate. I know both sides of that theological equation personally. Born and raised a Jew—in an interfaith home with a Jewish mom and a Catholic dad—I went to Reform Temple on Friday nights, Hebrew School one afternoon a week, and religious school on Sunday mornings. I was *bat mitzvah* at thirteen and confirmed at sixteen. At twenty-two I entered the Orthodox Jewish community. But at twenty-nine, a surprise vision of Jesus led me to seminary, baptism, ordination, church ministry, and a life of Christian discipleship.

But I'm getting ahead of myself. Let's get back to Jesus' question: "Who do you say that I am?" If that question had been posed to me before April 19, 1990, I wouldn't have known how to answer it. At least out loud. Until that day, he wasn't part of my life or my consciousness in any appreciable way. Up until that point, what I knew of Jesus was inferred from the history books. I knew about the Crusades. I knew about the torturous conversion of Jews during the Spanish Inquisition. I knew about pogroms, drunken mob attacks on Jews in Europe in the nineteenth and twentieth centuries. I knew about the Holocaust, the seeds of which were sown by Martin Luther, leader of the Protestant Reformation.[2] I knew about the dark chapters of Christian history in which my people, the Jewish people, had been treated cruelly by the church in Jesus' name. And what I knew, I didn't like. So, if the same question posed to the disciples had been posed to me, I would have felt awkward, embarrassed, angry. My answer would have been along the lines of "Jesus? He's the Christian God who hates Jews." Because of that misperception on my part, I kept my distance from him, just as I figured he was keeping his distance from me. We had a mutual agreement. Or so I thought.

Then came April 19, 1990, my twenty-ninth birthday, the day he came to me in a vision. I was meditating, fully awake, when all of a sudden, right before my eyes was Jesus. He didn't look like any of the pictures I had seen before. He wasn't blond-haired, blue-eyed, or fair skinned. And there was no name tag or caption that came with this vision. Nothing external to let me know who this was. Even so, every cell in my body knew: this was Jesus. He had thick, wavy, dark brown hair; a full dark brown beard; olive skin; dark eyes. Handsome, actually. Jewish, definitely. He never actually moved his lips or spoke out loud to me. His eyes said it all: *I understand you. I accept you. I love you.* His voiceless message came through loud and clear. Interestingly, he never asked me to understand him, accept him, or love him. He certainly didn't ask me to follow him. In fact, there were no strings attached. This was unconditional love and acceptance.

Now, as I think back on it, it brings to mind the song I would later learn in the black church community, a song about feeling the joy that comes from the touch of Jesus. "Something happened, and now I know, he touched me and made me whole."[3] But at the time, that's not how it felt.

In fact, it felt just the opposite. I was shocked, unnerved, unsettled. He spoke to me as if we had a relationship. As far as I knew we didn't. I was OK with that. Really OK with that. So, I wasn't sure what to do with this experience. My decision? Ignore it. Don't talk about it. Maybe it will go away. Maybe he will go away.

But it didn't. Neither did he. In fact, my curiosity about him only grew. And not speaking about this experience proved challenging. As discomfiting as it was for me to have had this vision of Jesus, it was even more discomfiting not to tell somebody. Especially for somebody like me who likes to talk about everything! I'm sure I managed to keep my mouth shut for at least a few hours.

Bursting, I confided in Rachel, a spiritual mentor. She would understand, I figured. She too had been raised in a home with one Jewish parent and one Christian parent.

"Did you know that Jesus was Jewish?" she asked when I told her about my experience.

"Yeah; everyone knows that."

"Well, did you know that his disciples were Jewish?"

"What's a disciple?" I asked. Funny question from a person about to become one. But what did I know from disciples?

"Oh," she said, light dawning, "you haven't read the New Testament?" It was more a statement than a question.

"It's not my book!" I responded with attitude.

"I'd better get you one," she said, as if she hadn't heard me.

She followed through, but I didn't. I didn't want to read the New Testament. For a Jew, this Jew anyway, it was anathema. Wouldn't that be like consorting with the enemy? It seemed like Christians had been at the forefront of every bad thing that ever happened to the Jews—from the time Jesus first showed up until the Holocaust—all with Jesus' stamp of approval, right?

As you're reading this, you probably get something I didn't at the time: the information I had was incomplete. In truth, I knew as little about contemporary Christians and Christianity as many Christians know about contemporary Jews and Judaism. From my current vantage point as a United Methodist clergyperson, I see that Jews are taught to mistrust Christians just as Christians are taught to mistrust Jews. Granted, we arrive at this mistrust from very different histories, but I think it's a problem. In fact, this mistrust gets at the crux of our problem. More on that in a bit.

Meanwhile, I didn't read the book Rachel bought me, but I did continue to process my Jesus experience with her. I even branched out and told several friends whom I thought were Christians. What they told me surprised me. They had longed for the kind of experience that I had had. As faithful Christians, they had prayed to receive the very message that had come to me—unbidden and undesired. I began to realize that my experience was fairly unusual. The pull to find out more about Jesus increased.

I Need to See for Myself

I found myself with a foot in two worlds: one foot in the Orthodox Jewish community—with its familiar focus on Torah, Sabbath, and commandments (*mitzvot*)—and the other foot in the strange new world of Jesus and his followers. Finally, I shared my unnerving experience with Reb Motti, my rabbi.

"Stay and learn with me," he urged. "We'll learn what the Talmud says about Jesus." That was a pretty generous offer from this Chassidic rabbi, as Talmud study was mostly reserved for men, and as far as I knew it didn't say much about Jesus.

"No," I shook my head, surprising even myself. "I need to go and see for myself." It wasn't the first time I had said those words: *I need to go see for myself.* Six years earlier I had said the same thing when I entered the Orthodox world from the much more liberal Reform Jewish community. At that time I had just returned home from a college-graduation trip to Israel, a gift from my mom's mother, on the Jewish side of the family, which ranged from Reform to Orthodox in their practice.

While we were in Israel, we had stayed with the Orthodox branch of the family: my Uncle Hillel and his wife and children. During those two weeks, I fell in love with Israel, Hebrew, and the experience of being Jewish. To be in the majority, rather than the minority, was a singular experience. Growing up Jewish in Fairfield County, Connecticut, was like being a bee in WASP country. White Anglo Saxon Protestant I wasn't. I never quite felt like I fit in.

After two weeks, my grandmother went back home to Denver and her work as the editor and publisher of a Jewish newspaper. But I convinced her to let me stay another two weeks. During that time, I wandered the streets of Jerusalem, found my way around the Old Shuk (Arab Market), visited museums, added to my rudimentary Hebrew, and soaked up the religious customs of my Orthodox Jewish family. One night, while sleeping on the cool stone tile floor in a borrowed army green sleeping bag, I had an awakening. Literally. I felt like God knocked on the side of my head, woke me up, and spoke to me. As I sat straight up in the sleeping bag, this thought came to me: "OMG, there is a God! And I have been living my life all wrong."

I had just graduated with a degree in environmental studies. Schooled in the sciences, I had an appreciation for the beauty of nature, but not for the divine wisdom behind it. Besides, like many young adults, my religious commitments wavered after I was confirmed. Forget about God; now I was into the party scene and guys! My life was not all it could be. It wasn't all I thought it should be. But from that moment on, I decided to learn more about my religion and to delve deeper into its teachings.

When the two weeks were up, I went back to Montpelier, Vermont, to the funky little apartment I rented (you had to walk through the bathroom to get to the kitchen or living room), and began to keep the Sabbath. I even brought my dishes down to the Winooski River to *kasher* them. (Think baptize.) I got more involved with my eclectic synagogue—a friendly mish mash of liberal and conservative Jews—helped lead *Shabbat* services, and began a Jewish women's group.

All the while, I read voraciously, studying the traditional teachings of Judaism. My non-Orthodox family was puzzled by this. But I threw off their concern and decided to see for myself about the Orthodox Jewish community. I then moved to Denver to be near family, the much larger Jewish community and a wonderful synagogue that welcomed Jews like me who were exploring a Torah-observant lifestyle (think born-again Jews).

The richness of the Sabbath,[4] the sense of community, the feeling of belonging, and the wisdom of the teachings all touched me deeply. Yes, there were sacrifices. I had to set aside my feminism to enter this community. Men and women were seated separately with a dividing curtain between them. Only men could be rabbis, lead prayer, and read from the Torah. Women had their sphere of influence, too, but not in the public ways I was used to. Yet, the sense of place and belonging, of history and tradition, of comfort and meaning was worth it to me at the time. I even married another *ba'al teshuvah* (returnee).

A year later, after being married in an Orthodox Jewish wedding ceremony—replete with the experience of each of us being lifted up on chairs and danced around and of setting up a kitchen with two sets of kosher dishes; one for daily use and the other for Passover—came this experience with Jesus. And I realized—sharply and reluctantly—that my spiritual journey was not over; my spiritual identity not yet fully defined. It was time for me to see for myself again. It was time to learn more about this Jesus.

Even though I didn't know what it said in the still unread New Testament Rachel had given me, Jesus' call to leave everything behind and come and follow him was what I ended up doing. I left behind all that was familiar and comfortable—community, customs, and as it turned out, my husband—to find out more about Jesus.

One and a half years after my Jesus experience, including one very awkward attempt at attending a Protestant church service—I felt so unsafe that I grabbed my purse every time we stood up and sat down—and one very confusing experience in a Messianic Jewish congregation—why did the women have their heads covered like Orthodox women and why were the men wearing *yarmulkes* (pronounced YAH-muh-kuhs; the *r* and *l* are silent) and why did they light three Sabbath candles instead of the usual two and why was the nice man trying to scare me into an immediate baptism?—after all this, I found myself walking through the doors of the Iliff School of Theology in Denver. *What's a nice Jewish girl like me doing in a place like this?* I thought. I certainly didn't plan on becoming a Christian, let alone a pastor. But there I was anyway, struggling to answer the question that all disciples are faced with: "Who do you say that I am?"

What's in a Name?

The biblical disciples had to ask themselves: Who is this Jesus who multiplies loaves and fishes, heals the sick with the touch of a hand or the fringes of a garment, gives sight to the blind and hearing to the deaf, and raises the dead? I had to wrestle with a question of a different sort. Who is this Jesus who comes, unasked, to a Jewish woman like me with understanding, acceptance, and love in his eyes? And why should I care?

When Jesus asked the disciples, "Who do people say that the Son of Man is?" they had a variety of answers. "Some say, John the Baptist, but others Elijah, and still others Jeremiah or one of the prophets." Yes, Jesus persisted, "but who do you say that I am?" "You are the Messiah, the Son of the living God," Simon Peter answered.[5] That took *chutzpah* to speak those words. The Jewish people had been waiting centuries for the Messiah to come. And for Simon to declare what his heart whispered—that took guts!

Jesus confirmed it: "Blessed are you, Simon son of Jonah! For flesh and blood has not revealed this to you, but by my Father in heaven."

And he tells him on that kind of faith the very church would be built. Then, Jesus changed Simon's name to Peter, the rock.[6]

Like Simon, I also went through a name change. Many a grocery store cashier has asked me about my name. Yes, it's very biblical. No, I wasn't born a Simon and then married a Peter. It was more intentional than that. In the Bible, a name change is often accompanied by a new purpose or a special interaction with God. Abram became Abraham, Sarai became Sarah, Jacob became Israel, and Simon became Peter. I was thinking about a new name that would embrace the new me.

As this process was unfolding, I went back to Rachel.

"Is there a Simon Peter in the Bible?" I asked, my New Testament still neglected on the bookshelf.

"Yes," she nodded.

"Was he a good guy or a bad guy?"

"A pretty good guy," she nodded again.

"Oh. That's the name that keeps coming to me." I finally cracked the book and went to read up on Simon Peter. I liked the idea of sharing a name with this Jewish follower of Jesus who also had his name changed. It fit.

But it wasn't just my last name that changed. Much as I loved my birth name, I laid it aside and took the name of the strong Jewish matriarch, Rebekah, who went against the customs of her time to embrace the new thing God was doing. Even though it went against the way things were done back then, she understood that her elder son Esau would serve her younger son, Jacob. I could relate to Rebekah's bravery because it seemed to me that this calling me from the Jewish community to Jesus and his followers was definitely going against the way things were done; at least in my world. But I also sensed, like Rebekah, that this break with tradition was God's doing. It surely wasn't mine! I could no more explain the vision of Jesus than I could explain it away. I just knew I wanted to go into it being clear about who I was: a Jew who was following Jesus.

Even though Peter and I bear the same name now, I was no rock in my faith at that point. More like a pebble! Yes, I was in seminary. But I still wasn't sure about this Jesus. Would it be safe to trust him? Would it be wise to cast my lot with his followers? Weren't these the same people who had caused so much pain and suffering for the Jews?

Eventually, through my studies in seminary and lots of inner wrestling, I came to answer Jesus' question like my namesake: You are the

Christ, the Messiah, Son of the Living God. But somewhere along the way, in both seminary and church, I noticed that the Jesus who came to me differed from the Jesus of the church, the local church anyway. The Jesus who came to me was Jewish. But the Jesus I heard about in church had been stripped of his Jewishness, divorced from his context, and turned into a Christian. A very nice Christian, but a non-Jew nonetheless. It's almost as if something had been lost in translation.

The more seminary courses I took, and the more church services I attended, the more I sensed it. It seemed to me that the Jews were the bad guys in every sermon I heard. Yes, even "Protestant liberalism has its own form of anti-Judaism: Jesus is gracious and against rules that exclude, with a backdrop that Jews are for rules and like to exclude."[7] I was mystified by the interpretive style that seemed to say the Old Testament existed to prove but one point: that the Jews had been given every chance to be faithful to God, had not risen to the challenge, and thus Jesus and the Christians came to save everybody! I chafed under that message. None of those interpretations fit the Judaism I had known or grown up with.

Like Mary, I pondered this in my heart. I wondered what to make of it. Over time, I began to collect books on the subject that might help me make sense of the disconnect I was experiencing. I wanted the church to experience the beauty of Judaism as I knew it and as I suspected Jesus must have known it. Slowly, I started to incorporate my findings into sermons and Bible studies, to lead Jewish Passover Seders in churches during Lent, and to introduce churches to other Jewish holidays. When I left local church ministry after fifteen years of pastoring, I took my findings on the road to give workshops in churches on reading the Bible through Jewish eyes. This book is the result.

In a nutshell, here's what I found. For the better part of two millennia, the Bible has been read and interpreted from the perspective that Judaism and Christianity were/are two entirely different belief systems, that the former has been replaced by the latter and that the inferior has been superseded by the superior. But when I read the Bible with Jewish eyes I found something else entirely. The first thing that became apparent to me is that Jesus was born a Jew, raised a Jew, lived a Jew, died a Jew, and was even resurrected a Jew. He was no backsliding Jew, but an observant Jew. He honored and observed the Sabbath and the Jewish holidays. But most of all, he honored and observed the Torah, the Hebrew Bible, or what Christians call the Old Testament. He quoted it, taught from it, lived it. Far from declaring it null and void, in some cases he even made it more demanding. I found that his best-loved teachings come straight out of it: You shall love the Lord your God with all your heart, with all your soul, and with all your strength (Mark 12:30 and Deuteronomy 6:5) and your neighbor as yourself (Mark 12:31 and Leviticus 19:18). Not that Jesus didn't challenge his people. Or call his people to new interpretations and radical recommitments. You bet he did! Just like the Jewish prophets who came before him. But I don't see that he ever stopped being Jewish.

Thinking of Jesus in this way has certainly changed my perspective. I once thought I had to shed my Jewishness to follow Jesus. No more. Instead I have adopted a wider embrace of the different spiritual streams that run together and feed me. I think of myself not as a convert from one religion to another, like someone who has exchanged one set of lenses for another, but rather a person who views the world through multiple lenses at the same time. It's a more richly nuanced, layered approach. That makes me something of a spiritual hybrid. The truth is, I think of myself as a Reform-Odox-Metho-Juda-Lic. Let me explain. I have been shaped by Reform and Orthodox Judaism, Methodism, and even a bit of the Catholicism of my father's side of the family. I'm the sum of all my parts. And more. I am working on understanding and healing the breach between Judaism and Christianity within me, and Jewish and Christian communities are doing the same. It's incredibly refreshing to move from a two-thousand-year stance of suspicion to one of creative appreciation and engagement. We are recognizing that our histories and destines are intertwined.

Jesus was Jewish—through and through. I believe it's important for the church to own that and to claim it proudly. You might say, like I did, "Yeah, everybody knows he was Jewish. So what?" Glad you asked! Here's the so what. I believe how we see, name, and claim Jesus has everything to do with how we see, name, and claim each other. According to one of my favorite books, *Good Goats: Healing Our Image of God*, "we become like the God we adore."[8] So, if we adore a good Christian Jesus who stood fiercely against the bad faithless Jews as I once thought, then it would follow that the church ought to do likewise. For centuries, that had been the church's practice—to the great detriment of all involved. But if we adore a Jesus who was a Jew through and through, then it would follow that the church ought to treat Jews with love, respect, and honor. Or as Pope John Paul II once said, as "our elder brothers."[9] This is becoming the church's new practice; to the great benefit of church and synagogue. As a result, Jewish-Christian relations have come a mighty long way.

But truthfully, we still have a ways to go. We still have an "us versus them" mentality that comes out of the mistaken image of a good Christian Jesus who stood against the bad faithless Jews. It translates into the almost unconscious idea that in order to stand with Jesus, we've got to stand against someone else. If not Jews, then maybe gays. Or Muslims. Or undocumented aliens. Or the poor. Or the rich. Or liberals. Or conservatives. Or Republicans. Or Democrats. Or even against other Christians. You name it: the list goes on and on. All in the name of Jesus. But what if Christianity is rooted not in the good Christian Jesus who stood against the bad faithless Jews, but in a Jewish Jesus who stands fiercely with and for his people—in love and in challenge? What if we as Christians saw ourselves as grafted in to this relationship . . . not as victors but as welcomed guests? That would change things. Instead of automatically turning a suspicious eye on everyone who is somehow different from us, we might just find ourselves standing fiercely with and for other people. We might find ourselves extending the same understanding, acceptance, and love that Jesus extends to us. No strings attached. What a gift this would be in our multicultural, multifaith, multiethnic, multilingual world! A gift that the world could desperately use. All in the name of the Jew named Jesus!

How do we get started? It all begins with how we answer the question that Jesus once asked, "Who do you say that I am?"

2. Was Jesus
a Christian?

During my second year in seminary, living in to my new name, I received the call to ministry. I felt God say to me, "I want you to lead my people." Intuitively I realized God meant his *Christian* people. This was a shocker of an announcement from God. I had never planned on becoming a Christian, let alone a Christian minister. But what do my plans have to do with anything?!

True to form, I fought God for a while on this. I remember sitting in the back row of my church history classes, debating with God. I wasn't at all sure I wanted to cast my lot with the church. Given the bad blood, historically, between Christians and Jews, it didn't seem like a wise move. "Are you sure about this?" I would say to God. "Can't you choose somebody else?" There wasn't much of an answer from God. I took that as a no.

I surrendered and accepted God's call. The trouble was I wasn't prepared for it. I had been attending seminary, but not church. I visited several churches but none of them really jazzed me. Then I was introduced to the pastor and people of Scott United Methodist Church, an African-American congregation that had put on a dynamic Martin Luther King, Jr., service at the Iliff School of Theology. Mary, one of the women from the church said to me on her way out of the building that night, "You should come visit our church some Sunday." I was thrilled with the invite. "Thank you. I believe I will." I had always wanted to attend a black church service, even as a kid. It seemed so lively, so interesting, so passionate.

I trooped off to Scott UMC the next Sunday and the next and the next and the next and the next and the next. I was hooked! The people were warm and welcoming. The music was inspiring. The choir was fabulous. The preacher was enthusiastic and kind. The congregation was responsive: "Amen!" and "Preach it!" could be heard throughout the sermon. I was part of this congregation first as a member then as a leader for the better part of five years.

Even so, I had culture shock. Yes, I was a drop of cream in a rich cup of coffee; I was one of the few non-African Americans at this church. But this culture shock wasn't so much about racial or ethnic differences. The need to deal with those cropped up later. It was the religious differences that got me. For two religions that have so much in common—Judaism and Christianity—the differences between the Orthodox Jewish community and the Protestant church were staggering.

Don't get me wrong. I met beautiful, giving, faithful people in the church whose lives were undergirded by deep prayer and faithful Bible study, joyous worship, tremendous acts of kindness and mercy, and courageous efforts at systemic change. I met inspiring men and women who gave freely of themselves to bless the less fortunate. I grew to love them with all my heart. Even so, I missed the rhythms of Jewish life. I missed the Sabbath whose leisurely pace was punctuated by special meals and table songs shared with friends and family, Sabbath worship services, rest, and study. I missed observing the Holy Days, with their special rituals, foods, and blessings. I missed saying prayers in Hebrew. I missed lighting candles and blessing wine to welcome in the Sabbath and festivals. I missed the majesty and sanctity of the Torah scrolls being carried from the Ark and around the congregation before being unrolled for the chanting of the week's Torah portion. As interesting and engaging as church was, I felt like a fish out of water. I missed my old life; I missed it all. Well, except for one thing.

I didn't miss keeping kosher. Most Reform Jews don't keep the full dietary laws; I found them difficult to get used to when I became Orthodox. For example, when I was first married, my then-husband and I set up housekeeping with four sets of dishes. Four! One set of meat dishes and one set of milk dishes for Passover, and another set of each for the rest of the Jewish year. That seemed like overkill to me. I never could really wrap my mind around it. It was one discipline I wasn't sorry to let go of.

The other spiritual practices were much harder to let go of. Yet, I was slipping out of the Jewish rhythms of life and study and worship that had come to define me. All to be with Jesus and his followers. Even as I was getting used to the Christian way of living with its own cadence of Sunday worship, Bible study, choir practice, mission work, and prayer meetings, I was trying to make sense of how Jesus and the New Testament understood Torah. The prevailing wisdom seemed to be that Christians were "freed" from the "burden" of the Law. As if the Torah was some terrible thing. For the most part, though, I didn't experience Torah or Jewish life that way at all. Yes, keeping kosher was tough for me. The separation of the sexes was tough for me too—but that was more custom than law. Besides I doubt those things would have been as tough two thousand years ago when the New Testament was being written.

So where did this idea of being set free from the burden of the Law come from? I didn't really know yet. But I was curious to see what Jesus had to say about the Law. As I searched the Gospels, the most striking thing I found was this:

> Do not think that I have come to abolish the law or the prophets; I have come not to abolish but to fulfill. For truly I tell you, until heaven and earth pass away, not one letter, not one stroke of a letter, will pass from the law until all is accomplished. Therefore, whoever breaks one of the least of these commandments, and teaches others to do the same, will be called least in the kingdom of heaven; but whoever does them and teaches them will be called great in the kingdom of heaven. For I tell you, unless your righteousness exceeds that of the scribes and Pharisees, you will never enter the kingdom of heaven.[1]

Wait a second! Here I have just left the rhythms and practices of Jewish life, and now Jesus is saying that Torah righteousness, Torah observance, and the kingdom of heaven are deeply intertwined? Maybe I should have cracked that New Testament a little bit earlier! It sure sounded to me like he called people to live a deeply Jewish life. Yet I looked around at the church and it didn't look or feel anything like the Jewish life I had just left behind. I was confused.

The more I searched the Scriptures, the more confused I got. First, I never realized that there was so much that was negative about Jews, Judaism, and the Law in the New Testament. Second, I had always thought of Jesus as more Christian than Jewish. Wasn't he the founder of Christianity? After reading the New Testament, I began to wonder if Jesus was really a Christian after all.

Was Jesus a Christian?

"Was Jesus a Jew? Was Jesus a Christian?" Those are the first two questions I pose when I lead workshops in churches on the Jewish roots of Christianity. About half the hands go up for Jewish. More go up for Christian. Several for both. A few aren't sure how to respond. Either way, lively discussion emerges. Kevin summed up what most people were thinking at one workshop when he said, "Of course he was a Christian. He's Jesus *Christ!*" Shawna added, "He *was* a Jew, but then he became a Christian."

That reminds me of a joke I once heard. One day, Zelda is talking to the LORD. "*Oy vey*, LORD, my heart is breaking. I'm not sure what to do. My son, my Bernie, has become like somebody I don't know. All of a sudden he tells me he has converted!" She sighs. "My Bernie has become a Christian." "*Nu*," commiserated the LORD. "Tell me about it. The same thing happened to my son!"

Was Jesus a Jew or a Christian or both or neither? How would you answer the question about Jesus' identity? I think It depends on how you define the terms *Jewish* and *Christian*. While countless volumes have been written on these identities, and much room exists for discussion and disagreement, let's go for the big picture.

Let's start with Jews and Judaism. Judaism is a religion, yes, but it's more than that. It also encompasses culture and ethnicity. All children born to a Jewish mother are automatically Jewish. Some Jewish denominations also recognize as Jews children born to Jewish fathers.[2] Jews by choice convert into Judaism. That's the baseline definition of who is a Jew. Some would add a belief in one God, connection to the Torah, and someone who follows the commandments of God.

What is a Christian? Definitions vary here too. A Christian has come to be seen as someone who is a baptized believer in Jesus and his teachings. Others would say a Christian is someone who believes in Jesus as their Lord and Savior. For the most part, people see these categories of Jewish and Christian as mutually exclusive: Christians believe in Jesus, Jews don't. Most Jews are born into the covenant with God; Christians must choose. Where does Jesus fit? To discover more about Jesus' identity, let's look at the record found in the Gospels, starting with his family and early life.

The Eighth Day of Christmas

First off, Jesus is definitely born to a Jewish mother, Mary. He's raised by two Jewish parents who are devoted to Jewish life. To affirm that, consider the eighth day of Christmas. Do you remember what happened that day? No, I'm not talking about eight maids a-milking. I'm talking about when Jesus is formally welcomed into the Jewish people. After he is born in a humble feeding trough, after the angels sing "Glory to God in the highest" and announce good news of great joy to all the people, after the shepherds, amazed, run to Bethlehem but before the Magi come bearing gifts, Jesus is circumcised and named.

From the days of Abraham, this ancient rite of circumcision has been a sign of the covenant with God. In fact, it's the first and most basic commandment or law (*mitzvah*) to be fulfilled for a Jewish baby boy. Circumcision is a permanent sign, etched in the flesh, of partnership with God.

> This is my covenant which you shall keep, between me and you and your offspring after you: Every male among you shall be circumcised. You shall circumcise the flesh of your foreskins, and it shall be a sign of the covenant between me and you. Throughout your generations every male among you shall be circumcised when he is eight days old.[3]

Jesus is circumcised and named[4] with "the name given by the angel before he was conceived in the womb."[5] But he's not the only Jewish boy whose circumcision and naming are noted in the New Testament. Even before he's born, his cousin John is welcomed into the covenant, also on the eighth day.[6] Perhaps even more than lineage and ancestry, circumcision anchored these boys and their families firmly in the Jewish community.

About a month after the circumcision, after Mary has observed the days of purification,[7] Mary and Joseph come to Jerusalem with Jesus. There they offer a sacrifice and consecrate him, as a firstborn, to the Lord. In addition to this reminder of the Exodus, Jesus, like all firstborn males, is "redeemed."[8] This is another ancient Torah practice. Joseph and Mary would have paid a small sum (five silver shekels in biblical times; today, usually five silver dollars) and then performed a brief ritual in the Temple to fulfill the commandment (*mitzvah*).

While the family is at the Temple, two righteous and devout Jews, Simeon and the prophet Anna, recognize Jesus as a sign of God's salvation and praise God, for this "light for revelation to the Gentiles and for glory to your people Israel" who would himself redeem Jerusalem.[9] They speak words of praise and blessing over him.

Something is hidden in plain sight here. Do you see it? From his earliest days, Jesus is raised in a strong and beautiful Jewish home. From circumcision to naming to offering a sacrifice to consecration and redemption, Mary and Joseph do "everything required by the law of the Lord."[10] Not from a sense of empty duty or obligation, I suspect, but from a profound connection to God and Torah and love of their child, Jesus.

After these commandments (*mitzvot*) are fulfilled, Jesus and his parents "returned to Galilee, to their own town of Nazareth." At home in Nazareth the commandments, blessings, prophesies, and praises take root: "the child grew and became strong, filled with wisdom; and the favor of God was upon him."[11] Jesus is raised in the Jewish religion by devout parents. But what happens as he gets older? Does he grow into it? Or, like so many other teenagers, does he lose interest and move on to other things?

Train Up a Child

Just as Christians celebrate Easter and Christmas every year, so Jesus and his family—along with their relatives and friends—celebrated Passover every year. It was a big to-do. Each spring in the Hebrew month of Nisan they trekked from their home in Nazareth up to Jerusalem for the seven-day festival of Passover.

One year, as Jesus was approaching manhood by traditional Jewish calculation, "when he was twelve years old, they went up as usual for the festival."[12] They may have gone up as usual but they didn't come back as usual. The rest of the family headed home but unbeknownst to them Jesus stayed behind in Jerusalem, without even a word. What Mary and Joseph would've given for a cell phone and a text message! Without any digital advantage however, his parents were worried sick. They turned around mid-journey and finally located Jesus in the Temple. They weren't that happy about it either. Mary scolds Jesus who was "sitting among the teachers, listening to them and asking them questions." Apparently, they were also asking Jesus questions because the teachers "were amazed at his understanding and answers." Jesus, unfazed, wonders why his parents were searching for him. "Did you not know that I must be in my Father's house?" His parents were as baffled by his actions and his response as Jesus was by their anxiety.[13]

If this story is any indication, Mary and Joseph definitely trained up their child in the way he should go.[14] He loved God, loved Torah, and loved learning—all pluses in the Jewish world view. As the years went by, "Jesus increased in wisdom and in years, and in divine and human favor."[15] Mary and Joseph did a good job raising Jesus as a faithful Jew. But as parents know all too well, not every kid keeps the faith. What about Jesus? Did he take it on as his own as he grew up? Or did he leave it behind and become a Christian?

My Son the Rabbi

I wonder if Mary and Joseph were as baffled by Jesus' career choice as they were by his twelve-year-old behavior. Or did they see it coming? Jesus was not destined to become a life-long carpenter, let alone a doctor. Rather, he was going to be a rabbi. One of the first stories of Jesus' adulthood takes place in the synagogue.[16] It seems he not only embraced his childhood faith, he became a teacher of it. In this story, he reads from the scroll of Isaiah, gives a talk, gains the admiration of the people, and later their ire. Courageously, he didn't back away from tough teachings.

Nor did he stay put in the synagogue or even a single town. He took his teachings on the road.

As he walked by the Sea of Galilee, he saw two brothers, Simon, who is called Peter, and Andrew his brother, casting a net into the sea—for they were fisherman. And he said to them, "Follow me, and I will make you fish for people." Immediately they left their nets and followed him. As he went from there, he saw two other brothers, James son of Zebedee and his brother John, in the boat with their father Zebedee, mending their nets and he called them. Immediately they left the boat and their father, and followed him.[17]

Have you ever wondered what made people drop everything and follow Jesus? I have. I used to think it was something about his voice, his words, or his presence. Or maybe the same kind of understanding, acceptance, and love I experienced from him. But unlike his appearance to me, there was a definite call here: "Follow me, and I will make you fish for people."

When we get a sense of Jewish practice in Jesus' day, this was not as unexpected as it might seem. Back then, many Torah teachers itinerated or traveled from place to place, teaching as they went. Their students or disciples would literally follow them around day after day to observe how they lived. Instead of announcing a Bible study at a set time and place as Bible teachers do today, rabbis passed on their understanding of Torah to their students as they lived, traveled, studied, and ate together. The students would observe how the rabbi handled everything from money to temptation to disagreement and do likewise. It's like the Methodist itinerancy on steroids; not only does the leader itinerate, so do the followers!

This first-century context lends new meaning to the words, "Go and make disciples of all nations," doesn't it?[18] For Jesus and other Torah teachers of his day, disciple-making was a hands-on venture that required one's whole being. No wonder Jesus advised his students to count the cost of discipleship. It was steep! One scholar notes that this itinerant teacher/student form of learning was the ancient equivalent of postdoctoral work; disciples could only manage it for three years.[19] After that they would go back to a more normal life.

The Kingdom of Heaven

As Jesus and his disciples traveled from place to place, they weren't alone. Other rabbis and their disciples were afoot in their own traveling classrooms. Jesus taught primarily about the Kingdom: "Repent for the kingdom of heaven is near."[20]

What is this kingdom Jesus spoke of? It was the Jewish hope of God's will being perfectly fulfilled. Jesus teaches his disciples how to pray for it: "Your kingdom come, Your will be done, on earth as it is heaven."[21] The kingdom wasn't just the subject of an occasional prayer or sermon. It was the heartbeat of Jesus' entire ministry.[22] Kingdom stories and teaching found their way into the Beatitudes and the Sermon on the Mount,[23] the Sermon on the Plain,[24] his many parables,[25] and the Last Supper.[26] Jesus saw it as his purpose in life, the very reason he was sent.[27] He preached about the Kingdom everywhere he traveled and healed people as a sign of its nearness.[28] Even resurrection didn't strip him of this message.[29] Nor did the message stop with him; he urged his disciples to proclaim it too. "As you go, proclaim the good news, 'The kingdom of heaven has come near.' "[30] So, Rabbi Jesus crisscrossed the Galilee with his disciples and their message of the Kingdom. Along the way they crossed paths with other teachers and their students. Common to all of them was the love of a good debate.

The Debate Team

Sometimes it seems as if around every bend someone was waiting to take down Jesus with an argument. But these tests weren't particular to Jesus. Nor were they ones he was necessarily meant to fail. Debate was a time-honored way teachers and preachers of the Law tested their wit, gained new insight into Torah, taught those around them, and honored God. In fact, as one observer notes: "In debating and disagreeing over the meaning of the Torah or how best to put it into practice, no rabbi felt that he (or his opponent) were in some way rejecting God or threatening Judaism; on the contrary, it was precisely through such arguments that the rabbis imitated and honored God."[31] That's the context for the story in which some Sadducees engaged Jesus on the topic of resurrection. Keep in mind that the Sadducees, unlike the Pharisees, rejected the idea of resurrection of the dead. They posed a Talmudic-type tale for Jesus to decipher.

"Teacher," they began, "Moses told us that if a man dies without having children, his brother must marry the widow and raise up offspring for him." They go on and tell a story that would challenge even the most agile rabbinic mind. "Now there were seven brothers among us. The first one married and died, and since he had no children, he left his wife to his brother. The same thing happened to the second and third brother, right on down to the seventh. Finally, the woman died. Now then, at the resurrection, whose wife will she be of the seven, since all of them were married to her?" Note the sign of respect with which they address Jesus, "Teacher," even as the story is designed to stump him. But Jesus doesn't miss a beat. Quicker than they, he replies with wit, verve, and a deep knowledge of the Scriptures. "You are in error because you do not know the Scriptures or the power of God. At the resurrection people will neither marry nor be given in marriage; they will be like the angels in heaven. But about the resurrection of the dead—have you not read what God said to you, 'I am the God of Abraham, the God of Isaac, and the God of Jacob'? He is not the God of the dead but of the living."[32]

Touché! The crowds loved his answer, especially the Pharisees. Score two points for Jesus. When they heard Jesus had "silenced the Sadducees," on the matter of resurrection, "they gathered together" to pose one of their own questions, "Teacher, which commandment in the law is the greatest?' "[33] Again, note the title of esteem: Teacher. The Pharisees weren't ganging up on him here. Instead, they saw in Jesus a worthy opponent. Who wants to debate someone who can't hold up their end?

What do we know so far about Jesus' identity? He was born and raised Jewish, trained up in the religion since his birth. He studied and taught Torah, he was a respected rabbi and teacher of the Law, and he was sharp-witted when it came to rabbinic debate. But perhaps as he developed his own disciples and interpretations of the Torah, he was becoming a Christian. Let's see, shall we?

The Laws of Love

"Which commandment in the law is the greatest?" The traditional count of commandments in the Torah is 613; these include laws about how to relate to God, family, neighbors, and community; life and death; war and peace. Laws about Sabbath and holy days are tucked in there with laws on food, work, and civil disputes. Winnowing the Torah down to its essence was a favorite pastime among some of the faithful.[34] Jesus answered without hesitation: "You shall love the Lord your God with all your heart, and with all your soul, and with all your mind." He names a second one as well: "You shall love your neighbor as yourself." He finishes with, "On these two commandments, hang all the law and the prophets."[35] Right about here is where my workshop participants pipe up. "Now see, here, this focus on love is what makes Jesus a Christian. Maybe he was a Jew before. But now he's definitely becoming a Christian."

I can understand that point. Jesus is definitely known for teaching love. But what's interesting is that this "Christian" teaching comes straight from the Torah. Remember the New Testament wasn't written yet; Jesus' Bible was the Jewish Bible, which Christians call the Old Testament. These passages he's quoting aren't obscure, little-known passages either. The first is from Deuteronomy 6:5 and the second is from Leviticus 19:18. Deuteronomy 6:5 is known as the *V'ahavta* ("you shall love"). This commandment is chanted, affirmed, and prayed at every Sabbath service and indeed every morning and evening during the daily set times of prayer. Interestingly, in Mark 12:28-31, Jesus begins his answer with Deuteronomy 6:4, "Hear, O Israel: the Lord our God, the Lord is one." This affirmation of faith places his answer even more firmly in the prayer life of the Jewish people. For the *Shema* ("hear"), the sentence that precedes the *V'ahavta*, is also recited during daily morning and evening prayer, and at other times in Jewish life. In keeping with Deuteronomy 6:6-9, the *Shema* and *V'ahavta* are inscribed on parchment, slipped into a decorative case, and affixed to the doorposts of Jewish homes. Known as a *mezuzah* (doorpost), it is the sign of a Jewish home. You could say Jesus' teaching on love comes right out of the heart of Judaism. Or even better, the fringes.

What Would Jesus Do?

Do you remember the story of the hemorrhaging woman who reaches out to Jesus for healing? She's been bleeding for twelve long years. She's used up all her money on doctors who can't help. Now she's desperate. As Jesus is on his way to heal another woman, she reaches out her hand to touch him—or his cloak—well, the fringe of his cloak to be exact. "If I only touch his cloak I will be made well," she thinks to herself. And so she reaches out from behind to touch the hem of his garment.[36] But why touch the edge of Jesus' clothing? You've probably heard sermons that she had to be secretive because she was a woman and she couldn't approach Jesus from the front for fear of being cast away, or because she was ritually impure due to her bleeding. As a supposed second-class citizen, she would have to content herself with a slight brush against his clothing. Perhaps.[37] But those interpretations miss the point. To read this passage with Jewish eyes is to understand what would have been on the hem or edge of his outer garment. Jesus wore, as did all the Jewish men of his day, fringes (*tzitzit*) in accordance with the Torah command found in Numbers 15:37-41.

> The LORD said to Moses: "Speak to the Israelites, and tell them to make fringes on the corners of their garments throughout their generations and to put a blue cord on the fringe at each corner. You have the fringe so that, when you see it, you will remember all the commandments of the LORD and do them, and not follow the lust of your own heart and

your own eyes. So shall you remember and do all my commandments and you shall be holy to your God. I am the LORD your God who brought out of the land of Egypt, to be your God; I am the LORD your God."

Amy Jill-Levine, the noted Jewish New Testament scholar, wryly notes the fringes Jesus wore were the ancient Jewish equivalent of what many of his own disciples wear today: a WWJD bracelet.[38] The fringes serve as a reminder of God, covenant, and commandments. When the hemorrhaging woman reached out her hand to touch those fringes it was her way of connecting not only with the holy rabbi of God but the holy Torah and the commandments of God. She wasn't touching the least important part of his clothing but the most important part. C'mon people, this was a woman with *chutzpah*, confidence, faith. She was gutsy! Jesus certainly rewards her actions: her faith evokes healing as power goes out from him.

Are you seeing what I began to see as I searched the Scriptures? Jesus is deeply grounded in Jewish life from birth through adulthood. He becomes a rabbi, calls disciples, proclaims the most Jewish of hopes in word and deed, clothes himself in the commandments, teaches Torah, attends synagogue, honors the Sabbath as a time of rest from work, and observes the Jewish holidays. He's a Jew. In fact, the word *Christian* didn't even exist during his day. For the bulk of Christian history, however, Jesus has been seen as a Christian, the ultimate Christian. Yet he couldn't very well follow himself. Certainly he believed in his own teachings, but even they were Jewish. His reliance on God was without question.

Was Jesus a Christian? No more than Martin Luther was a Lutheran or John Wesley was a Methodist. Like Jesus, Wesley was a man around whom a new religious movement began. Wesley never disavowed being an Anglican priest. Nor did Jesus ever disavow his Judaism. Both, however, pushed the edges of their faith. Here's the way I see it: Judaism was the religion of Jesus while Christianity is the religion about Jesus.

So if Jesus, who from the moment of his birth to his death and beyond was Jewish—why isn't the church more Jewish in practice? Why aren't Christians actually Jewish? In the next chapter we'll explore this more as we address the question: Did the Jews reject Jesus?

3. Did the Jews Reject Jesus?

Both/And

Ispotted Bernerd at a workshop I was giving at a local church. The *yarmulke* on his head was a dead giveaway. Clearly Jewish. I went up and introduced myself thinking he was a rabbi from a nearby temple. Even as I approached him I wondered if I needed to be on guard. Or defend myself. A dual identity like mine is not well accepted in much of the Jewish community. There are at least three reasons for this. First, as one Jewish acquaintance said to me recently: "Look, you're either a Jew or a Christian. You can't be both." I, of course, used to think the same thing. "Jews don't believe in Jesus. Christians do. They're two entirely different religions." I could finish the argument for him; I know how it goes. He's absolutely right of course; and not a little bit wrong. More on that later. Second, Jews are understandably afraid that the Jewish community, as small as it is, might disappear altogether through conversion, assimilation, or apathy. Jews are currently a scant 2 percent of the US population; that number is down from previous decades. Third, the long, sordid history of Christian anti-Semitism has made Jews wary of Christianity. Understandably so, but tragic nonetheless. Jews confuse Jesus with the terrible things that have been done to our people in his name.

As Bernerd began to speak, I realized he felt much the same way as I did. Wondering if he needed to defend himself to me. As a Jew, he had a vision of Jesus that changed his life. In some ways good, and in some ways not so good. After the vision, he began hanging out with Christians. But they didn't really get his Jewish practice. He also hung out with Jews. But they were uncomfortable with the whole Jesus thing. He found himself suspended between two communities. Part of both without fully fitting into either one. I could relate. It's been twenty-three years since my own vision of Jesus changed my life. I'm still not quite fully at home in either the Jewish community or the church.

Here's what I mean. One Friday per month I join the little Reform Jewish community of *Kol Ha'Am,* "Voice of the People," for *Shabbat* dinner. Surrounded by churchy posters on the walls of the Lutheran church where we meet, we light the Sabbath candles, say the blessing over wine, and give thanks for the fresh baked *challah* (pronounced KHA-lah) in Hebrew and English. Then we share a potluck dinner, relax, and visit. At Passover we hold a Seder; at Rosh Hashanah and Yom Kippur we have services, discuss Torah, and blow the shofar; at Chanukah we light the Menorah and eat potato latkes. It's a great little community; they have welcomed my Catholic husband and me with open arms. But it's still a micro version of what I long for—more Torah study, more Jewish spirituality, more Hebrew, and definitely more singing. Even so, it is Jewish community and it feeds my soul.

In the years following my departure from the Orthodox Jewish community, I attempted to welcome in the Sabbath on my own. Even as I felt more connected to the Jewish community, though, it underscored my solitariness. Judaism is meant to be lived communally. Now being part of this Jewish community I feel a greater wholeness.

The interesting thing is I'm not the only minister there. Lynn, who pastors a large Presbyterian church, has been coming for years. Her husband, Dan, is the regular *Kol Ha'Am challah*-baker. Other non-Jews, too, are a regular part of this community. Perhaps the rituals of challah, wine, and candles feed them too. Or maybe it's just the friendship and the latkes.

As long as I've been teaching Christians about the Jewish roots of Christianity, I have met Jews and Christians alike who are drawn into the overlapping space where Judaism and Christianity intersect. Some Christians are on their way to becoming Jews. Some Jews are becoming Christians. Others like me and Bernerd have a foot in each world, our hearts embracing a larger space than either faith tradition alone encompasses. Many Christians long to live more like Jesus and his disciples did. They want to experience something of the religion <u>of</u> Jesus, and not just the religion <u>about</u> Jesus. Or they are intrigued by the biblical holidays and holy days mandated by God in the Torah and wonder why Christians don't observe them anymore.

I can relate. I had let go of much of my Jewish practice, thinking it incompatible with Christian teaching. In fact, I was urged to do so by my earliest mentor in the faith. Honestly, I wish I hadn't listened. Now, the longer I follow Jesus, the more I reclaim my own Jewishness. If he was fully Jewish, why shouldn't I be? Why can't I be?

This *Rosh Hashanah* (Jewish New Year), I quietly left my office, gave Ann, my staff person, the rest of the day off, and went to Jewish New Year services at *Kol Ha'Am*. Same thing on *Yom Kippur*, the Day of Atonement. Together we prayed and sang and discussed Torah. I even got to help lead the singing. It was deeply satisfying to approach God in this way. I found the prayers intellectually challenging and spiritually fulfilling. I felt quietly jubilant.

Yet, this matter of feeding the soul is complicated business. Even as I'm with the people of *Kol Ha'Am*, I know that's not all it takes for me to be fully spiritually alive. Much as I love the Hebrew, the sacredness of *Shabbat,* the holidays, and belonging to the chosen covenant community that extends back thousands of years, I also love Jesus, the stories about the miracles he performed, his resurrection from the dead, and the devoted community that has gathered around him. I am also shaped by his announcement of the coming kingdom of God and the community that takes that future seriously. Above all, I can't forget Jesus' personal visitation to me: his understanding, acceptance, and love.

Loving and Hating Church

I have a countercultural confession to make: I am not one of those people who is spiritual but not religious. I am happily spiritual *and* religious. I suspect that puts me in the minority these days. I love a good religious service, especially if it's biblically based, intellectually challenging, and spiritually robust. The United Methodist Church, in which I'm ordained, often gets those things right. Although not always.

In my ministry, I have the opportunity to be in a lot of different churches. I love it. Up until the New Testament is read and the sermon is preached, that is. That's when my shoulders inch up toward my ears and I feel the tension build. Will Jews be made to seem faulty—religiously, spiritually, morally, ethically, historically—one more time? Will the preaching be anti-Jewish as a counterpoint to the righteousness of Jesus? I've heard sermons like this more times than I can count. I'm sorry to say that in the past I've even preached them myself. That was before I realized how I was falsely separating the Jew Jesus from his own Jewish people.

This "compare and contrast" method of preaching sets up a dishonest dichotomy. It sets against an inclusive, loving, good (Christian) Jesus from an exclusive, narrow-minded, legalistic (Jewish) people. It's an interpretive style so ingrained that otherwise good, sensitive preachers stretch to make strained comparisons. In one sermon I heard, the Temple priest Zechariah, father of John the Baptist, whom Luke describes in glowing terms, was compared to Scrooge and found faulty in faith. Just to make Jesus look good. In another, Jesus was portrayed as being for the people he healed but against the purity laws because they are exclusive. The preacher was moving toward a good point of including others who are different from you. But she got Jesus and his people wrong by reading twenty-first-century cultural values into an ancient society that accepted these values of purity and impurity.

The Pharisees are the subject of many of these compare and contrast sermons. They have been so often preached as shortsighted, small-minded, religious frauds who cared only about control that the term has become synonymous with hypocrite. Just look it up in the dictionary. To be sure, some of the Pharisees were hypocrites. Even rabbinic writings acknowledge that. Some of them tried to entrap Jesus and some wanted him dead. Jesus rightly called them on it. But other Pharisees sincerely sought him out,[1] warned him of danger,[2] appreciated his teaching,[3] extended hospitality even when being attacked by him,[4] and argued for open-mindedness.[5]

Painting all Pharisees with the same broad brush stroke is a problem. Stereotypes don't stay put in the past; they creep into the present. Hypocritical Pharisees come to represent Jews while Jesus comes to represent Christians. At a recent church workshop I taught, one businessman spoke up saying that in his circles being called Christian or Christlike was a compliment of the highest order. When I asked him, he admitted being called Jewlike would be an insult. "But if Jesus was a Jew," I pressed, "aren't *Christlike* and *Jewlike* synonymous?" The group laughed self-consciously, shifting in their seats as they contemplated this awkward juxtaposition. We have to stop promulgating anti-Jewish stereotypes. They hurt people. And they keep people away from the truly good news we have to offer. They kept me away for years.

That some of the Pharisees were hypocritical meant only that they fell short of their own high standards. That Jesus noticed and cared says volumes about his loving stand for the Jewish community and his shared commitment to righteousness. In calling out these Pharisees, he was a fierce advocate for them. Now wouldn't *that* make for an interesting sermon?

Bottom line: Much as I love the church, I grow weary of the righteousness of Jesus being artificially set over and against the long-ago Jewish community that successfully birthed him, raised him, taught him, and sent him on his way. It gets old. I long for the affirmation of Jesus to be connected with an affirmation of his own Jewish people. In truth, I long for him to be rightfully restored to his Jewish people, both in church and in synagogue.

So for all its limitations, I'm a both/and. I'm both a member of the Jewish people and of the community that follows Jesus. Today, that's a bit more complicated, controversial even, than it was in Jesus' day.

Jesus and His Jewish Followers

The first Christians were Jews. If it weren't for his Jewish followers, the memory and mission of Jesus would have died out a long time ago. As we have seen, Jesus was born a Jew, raised a Jew, lived the life of an itinerant rabbi with his own disciples, taught from Jewish texts, observed the Jewish Sabbath and other Jewish holy days, and died a Jew. As we'll see in Chapter 5, he was even resurrected a Jew.

Not only was Jesus Jewish, but so were his closest disciples and almost all of his first followers. In fact, the whole movement was decidedly Jewish. It wasn't until after his death that the movement spread to include a large number of Gentiles. Well into the fourth century and in some places longer, there were Jewish followers of Jesus who practiced Judaism, retaining their Jewish identity.[6]

Jesus' students included a wide diversity of Jews. Best known are two sets of brothers who left their fishing nets to say yes to Jesus' call: "Follow me and I will make you fish for people."[7] First there was Simon, whose Greek name was Peter, and his brother Andrew. Then there were the brothers James and John. Hailing from the same region of Galilee as Jesus, these fishermen are often thought to be rough and un-schooled. Rough, yes, but perhaps not unschooled.

In Jesus' time and beyond, Galilee was a vibrant center of Jewish learning.[8] Every community had a synagogue.[9] Many Pharisees, known in Jewish literature as sages or Masters of Torah, lived there[10]; others visited. These sages taught Torah inside and outside: in the academy, in gardens, under trees, and in marketplaces.[11] This leads me to wonder if Simon, Andrew, James, and John were already interested students of Torah. Would they have given up everything for the challenging life of following an itinerant rabbi otherwise? Andrew, according to the Gospel of John, was already a disciple of John the Baptist before switching his attention to Jesus.[12] The other three brothers would later become pillars of the Jerusalem church.

In addition to the fishermen, there were other devout Jews who followed Jesus. John's Gospel names a prominent Pharisee, Nicodemus, who calls Jesus "Rabbi," a title of respect, saying "we know that you are a teacher who has come from God."[13] After Jesus' death, other unnamed Pharisees are part of the community who follow Jesus.[14]

Jesus, Pharisees, and Fences

Not only did Pharisees follow Jesus, but Jesus followed the Phari-sees. Hard to believe, I know, given the contentious relationship Jesus had with some of them. Even as he calls them on hypocrisy,[15] he also acknowledges their righteousness[16] and their teachings: "The teachers of the law and the Pharisees sit in Moses' seat. So you must obey them and do everything they tell you."[17]

What is it the Pharisees did? They were a progressive lay movement who wanted "to renew and extend the observance of Jewish practice in society."[18] To increase people's sensitivity to holiness, they "made a fence around the law."[19] In other words, they established behavioral boundaries around God's commandments. That way, you could be sure of not sinning by refraining from the things that lead you to sin.

I can appreciate that. Eating sugar is sinful for me. Once I start, I don't easily stop. It's not a pretty sight! My mind and my spirit stray from God in a hurry. All I can think of is the next sweet thing to eat. It took me a long time to figure out how to avoid getting entangled with sugar. Over time I realized that every time I drink green tea, supposedly healthy for me, it eventually leads me to drink decaf coffee. Decaf coffee sets off a craving in me for the real thing. Drinking coffee with caffeine makes me want chocolate. Even naturally sweetened chocolate makes me want sugar. And lots of it. I've discovered if I don't want to battle sugar, all I have to do is stay away from green tea. It works like a charm.

The Pharisees used a similar method. And so did Jesus.[20] Consider the "fence" he made around several of the Ten Commandments. "You shall not murder," he agreed. But while you're at it, resist getting angry, don't hurl insults, don't even give in to contempt. One leads to the other and they all have the same outcome.[21] Likewise, he taught, "you shall not commit adultery." Therefore, don't even tempt yourself by looking at a woman lustfully. Believe me, you don't want those kind of wandering eyes in your head or groping hands on your arms. Better to be without them than to give in to sin.[22]

It makes sense that the learned, like the Pharisees, would be attracted to the teachings of Jesus. Jesus clearly knew his stuff. He shared some of the same aims as Pharisees. But Jesus' students also included Jews who didn't have nearly so much in common with Jesus or with each other. In fact, it was probably a stretch for them to get along.

A Diversity of Disciples

Matthew, a tax collector, would have been just the sort of person a Pharisee would have trouble with. While Pharisees focused on ethical living and were "champions of human equality,"[23] tax collectors were Robin Hoods in reverse. They took from the poor to give to the rich. They collaborated with Rome to collect the heavy taxes demanded by the state from their fellow Jews, many of whom were poor. When you think *tax collector*, don't think *civil servant* like an Internal Revenue Service employee. Tax collectors were rightly grouped with the sinners with whom they're often identified, as "those who violate familial and community welfare."[24] Add to the mix Simon the Zealot, a political revolutionary. Zealots were Jewish rebels who fought against Rome during the Jewish uprising in A.D. 66–70. Perhaps Matthew and Simon the Zealot would have found themselves at odds too. Matthew worked for the Roman system; Simon worked against it. Matthew tore down the values of the Jewish community; Simon actively defended them.

It wasn't just Jewish men who followed Jesus; this was an egalitarian movement. Jewish women had a strong place in it also. Jesus taught them and healed them. They in turn fed, funded, housed, and supported Jesus and his students. Even though they're not mentioned, who do you think cooked the Passover meal known as the Last Supper? Fifty days after his death, a group of Jesus' friends and followers were gathered in an upper room, immersed in prayer, waiting for the "promise of the Father" Jesus had spoken of. The twelve disciples were there as were "certain women."[25] I imagine this group included women like Mary Magdalene, and Mary the mother of James, and Salome. Not to mention Joanna and Susanna, and the other women who financially supported the movement.[26] Martha and Mary may have been present, too; their home in Bethany wasn't far from Jerusalem.[27]

Most telling were the members of Jesus' own family who were also present. His mother Mary was there and his brothers.[28] Sadly, no mention is made of Jesus' sisters; I like to think of them as there among the unnamed women.

Stand back a second and consider the question again: Did the Jews reject Jesus? The answer is obvious. Not these Jews. In fact, their faith is memorialized in the New Testament. Nine of the twenty-seven books of the New Testament are named after them. Several more are attributed to them. From the twelve apostles to women supporters to members of Jesus' own family, a broad swath of society was represented by these persons. Even Peter, who had denied knowing him just a few weeks earlier, was restored to a position of leadership. Already much larger than the original twelve, this group of Jewish followers is about to multiply yet again.

An International Following

Listen to what happens as we pick up the story from Acts 2. As Jesus' followers continued to pray, "[they] were filled with the Holy Spirit and began to speak in other languages, as the Spirit gave them ability." At the same time, "devout Jews from every nation under heaven" who were "living in Jerusalem" overheard them. I suppose it would have been hard not to. Accompanying their voices was "a sound like the rush of a violent wind" which filled the whole house they were in, not just the upper room. "Tongues, as of fire, appeared among them, and . . . rested upon them."[29]

While these men and women were declaring the deeds of God in Hebrew, the international crowd of Jews heard them as if they were speaking in *their* respective languages. They hailed from parts of Israel, North Africa, Europe, Asia, and Arabia. There were even islanders from Crete. They had all come to Jerusalem for the second of three pilgrimage festivals outlined in the Torah: Pentecost *(Shavuot)*. There to commemorate the giving of the Torah on Mount Sinai, they were doubly blessed as they witnessed the giving of the Holy Spirit.[30]

Pentecost is often called the birthday of the church. We sometimes think this is the moment that Jews converted, became Christian, organized the first church, hired a pastor, and had a potluck supper. It didn't go quite like that. They were deeply changed, but they didn't leave Judaism. In fact, they saw this outpouring of the Spirit as the fulfillment of a Jewish prophecy.

Peter, turning a moment of chaos into an opportunity to preach, reminds everyone present that Jesus, a teacher beloved by the crowds, had performed many signs and wonders. Yet he had been crucified. He reminds them, none too gently, of the part they played in it. But he goes on to say that Jesus didn't stay dead. Instead, God had freed him from death and made him both Lord and Messiah. This outpouring of the Spirit, once prophesied by Joel, was a sign that the last days, the messianic age, had indeed arrived.[31] Devastated by their sin, the Jews asked "What should we do?" Peter called them to turn back to God. If they would be baptized[32] in Jesus' name, they would be saved and assured of God's forgiveness. In fact, they would receive a tremendous gift, the crowning sign that the last days had indeed arrived. The gift of the Holy Spirit, once reserved only for kings and prophets, would now be poured out on all kinds of people. Three thousand Jews said yes.[33]

Do you see what's happening? Instead of breaking away from Judaism, these Jews are diving deeper into it. And it wasn't just the original three thousand that followed Jesus: "Day by day the Lord added to their number those who were being saved."[34]

Thousands of Jews Believe

One day, not long afterward, Peter and John went to the Temple for the afternoon prayer. While they were there, a disabled man was carried in. It was part of his daily routine; he showed up every day so he could beg for alms. When he asked Peter and John for money, he got a surprising answer. "I have no silver or gold, but what I have I give you; in the name of Jesus Christ of Nazareth, stand up and walk." When Peter bent down to help him up, the man's lame feet and ankles were healed. "Jumping up, he stood and began to walk, and he entered the temple with them, walking and leaping and praising God."[35] This was just the kind of miracle associated with the reign of God.[36]

The crowd of Israelites gawked. Peter, never one to pass up an opportunity for preaching, clued them in on what was happening. "The God of Abraham, the God of Isaac, and the God of Jacob,[37] the God of our ancestors has glorified his servant Jesus." He reminded them of their unfortunate role in Jesus' crucifixion. But he said, "By faith in his name, his name itself has made this man strong." He called them to repent and turn back to God so that they would be refreshed and restored. Peter and John were later arrested by the Sadducees for preaching the resurrection of the dead. But that didn't stop five thousand more Jews from becoming followers of Jesus.[38]

Are you keeping count? We've pushed past eight thousand Jewish believers. Meanwhile, the number continued to grow by leaps and bounds, including great numbers of men and women,[39] priests,[40] many thousands of believers, all zealous for the Law,[41] and even leaders of the Jewish people.[42] Add it up: there are thousands and thousands of Jews following Jesus. Discovering all of this made me realize I am far from alone. The New Testament is full of people just like me: both/ands, Jewish followers of Jesus.

Did the Jews reject Jesus? Far from it. As historian Dagobert D. Runes once noted, "The Jews were the makers of Christianity, from Jesus to Paul, and not its destroyers."[43] Truth be told, some were both destroyers and makers.

Saul: About as Jewish as You Can Get

Saul was one such man. A devout Jew, he persecuted followers of Jesus in an attempt to destroy the church. Breathing murderous threats, he was intent on destroying them.[44] A surprise encounter with Jesus on the road to Damascus changed all that.[45] He became the church's most famous leader. Better remembered by his Greek name Paul than his Hebrew name Saul, he became an apostle for Jesus—first to the Jews and then to the Gentiles.

I always thought Paul converted to Christianity. He was my "model" for what became of Jewish followers of Jesus. But again I began to search the Scriptures. Even though much of what he said confused me (more on that in Chapter 5), one surprising thing shone through: Paul remained a committed Jew. Even after his "conversion," when he speaks of being a Jew, it's in the present tense, not the past.

> I am a Jew, born in Tarsus in Cilicia, but brought up in this city at the feet of Gamaliel, educated strictly according to our ancestral law, being zealous for God, just as all of you are today.[46]

> Brothers, I am a Pharisee, a son of Pharisees.[47]

> I myself am an Israelite, a descendant of Abraham, a member of the tribe of Benjamin.[48]

As I searched the Scriptures more, I saw that Paul, too, regularly attended synagogue, read and taught from the Torah, and engaged his fellow Jews in deep theological discussion on the nature of the Messiah, resurrection of the dead, and other Jewish beliefs.[49] He was proud of being a Jew.[50]

I also saw that not everyone believed this. Once on a trip to Jerusalem, the elders told Paul that somehow word had gotten around that he was counseling Jews to let go of Torah.

> They have been told about you that you teach all the Jews living among the Gentiles to forsake Moses, and that you tell them not to circumcise their children or observe the customs.[51]

I would expect Paul to speak his mind if that were the case. He wasn't a person who held back. But he says nothing. The elders lay out a plan. They want Paul to take four Jewish men who had consecrated themselves to God under a Nazirite vow and help them complete it.[52]

> Join these men, go through the rite of purification with them, and pay for the shaving of their heads. Thus all will know that there is nothing in what they have been told about you, but that you yourself observe and guard the law.[53]

Still no word of objection from Paul. Quite the opposite, in fact.

> Paul took the men, and the next day having purified himself, he entered the temple with them, making public the completion of the days of purification when the sacrifice would be made for each of them.[54]

I suppose Paul's compliance shouldn't be a surprise. Not only does he complete his own Nazirite vow to God while at Cenchreae,[55] he helped Timothy get circumcised since his own father, a non-Jew, had not.[56] Long after Paul "converts," he was still eager to be in Jerusalem for the pilgrimage festival of Pentecost (*Shavuot*);[57] he even observed the fast on the Day of Atonement (*Yom Kippur*).[58]

Even with his strong Jewish commitments, and his ability to argue passionately, Paul was much more successful among the Gentiles than the Jews. He planted and cultivated a great many churches all over Asia Minor. So while the church was growing by leaps and bounds in Jerusalem with Jews, it was also growing greatly in Asia Minor with Gentiles. That presented some problems in the church: How to integrate Jews and non-Jews, with their varying customs, expectations, and background, into one community. As both Bernerd and I could tell you, from our own experiences, this was gonna take some work.

Must Gentiles Become Jewish in Order to Follow Jesus?

As a pastor, I was privileged to be a witness to people's deepest concerns. Many people have confided in me their fear for those who don't believe in Jesus. Will they be saved? Will they go to heaven? Will they enjoy the favor of God? They were especially concerned for Jews. I'll share my thoughts on this later in the book. Right now, consider this: Back in the day, followers of Jesus were asking a different question with different implications. Don't Gentiles need to become Jewish first in order to follow Jesus?

Startling at first, the question makes sense when considered more deeply. If Jesus, a Jewish rabbi was the Messiah—a Jewish redeemer of the Jewish people, attested to in the Jewish Scriptures—shouldn't Gentiles have to become Jewish first, and be in covenant with the God of Israel, in order to be a bona fide follower of Jesus and enter into the reign of the Jewish God he preached about?

As I mentioned before, when I entered seminary, I had no intention of becoming a Christian, let alone a Christian minister. I was a Jew following Jesus—no more, no less. I was there—like the God-fearer of old—to listen, to learn, to absorb—but certainly not to convert. Then came a day I did not foresee, the day God called me into ministry. "I want you to serve my people," God whispered somewhere deep inside me. I knew, from the context, that "serve" meant minister to and "my people" meant the Christian community. *Shoot!* I thought, *I'm not even going to church. Let alone baptized.*

I had attended services in the school chapel, even coming forward once to receive communion. My fellow student Alta had been leading the service that day and she said that ALL were welcome to come forward to participate. Likening the cup and bread to the Sabbath wine and challah, I went up as a Jewish follower of Jesus. But that was it. Now I heard this call from God. I was going to have to go all the way. There would be no getting around it. If I was going to serve God's people in the church, I would have to be fully identified with them. That meant baptism and church membership.

In the same way, those first Jewish followers of Jesus wrestled with what full identification with Jesus, the Jewish God, and the Jewish people would mean for non-Jews. It's no surprise that many insisted on circumcision—the sign of Israel's covenant with God.[59] That's why some Jewish believers had said to Gentile believers, "Unless you are circumcised according to the custom of Moses, you cannot be saved."[60] Although Paul and Barnabas disagreed heartily with them, these unauthorized teachers weren't the only ones who insisted on circumcision. Some Pharisees concurred, "It is necessary for them to be circumcised and ordered to keep the law of Moses."[61] In other words, they were of the opinion that Gentiles must first become Jewish in order to follow Jesus and enter into the reign of God.

The Jerusalem Council

Do Gentiles have to become Jewish in order to follow Jesus? This turned out to be a big question in the early church. Big enough that the elders and apostles called a meeting in Jerusalem to hash it out. In what came to be known as the Jerusalem Council,[62] Peter, Barnabas, and Paul each spoke movingly about how God was working among the Gentiles.

Finally, James, the head of this messianic subset of the Jewish community, offered his decision. Considering the words of the prophet Amos, James believed that this was the time Amos once prophesied about in which "all other peoples may seek the Lord—even all the Gentiles."[63]

Don't misunderstand. It's not that Gentiles weren't allowed to seek the Lord in previous times. Rather, it's that pagans worshiped many gods—all at the same time. Their seeking out of Israel's one God, and Israel's God pouring out the Spirit on them as well, signaled that something brand new was happening. James realized that since these Gentiles had already been exposed to the Law of Moses from regular synagogue attendance, they were likely already doing their best to follow it. No need to make them take on the whole covenant. Instead, they would just need to adhere to the basic morality asked of all Gentile God-fearers,[64] "abstinence from idolatry, sexual immorality and murder."[65] With these in place Gentiles could be peacefully integrated into the Jewish community. At least according to Acts. Galatians 2:1-14 tells the story from a different point of view. It's not quite as harmonious. Yet the result is the same: Gentiles do not need to become Jewish in order to follow Jesus and enter into the reign of God.

Jeannie had been listening carefully during one of my workshops. She was closely following what the Scriptures said about Jesus being Jewish. Plus all the disciples. Even Paul. People she had long thought were Christian. She took copious notes. Finally, she voiced a question. "Shouldn't we be Jewish too?" she asked, with a real openness in her voice. The answer for Gentiles today is the same as it was back then. Come as you are to the kingdom of God, for "God shows no partiality."[66] Here's what I find interesting about all of this. The fact that this question mattered so much two thousand years ago and that it matters today, underscores the deeply Jewish nature of the early church.

Why Didn't All Jews Believe in Jesus?

By now you may be wondering: How come all Jews didn't believe in Jesus? There were many Judaisms at the time of Jesus; each with their own understanding of what it meant to be faithful to God and the covenant. Following Jesus was one way. But there were others. There were a variety of Torah teachers on the scene each in their own traveling classroom. Additionally, some Jews followed the Pharisees, others the

Sadducees, and others the community of the Essenes at the Dead Sea. And who knows how many never actually heard of Jesus during his lifetime?

Of those who did, some simply didn't believe Jesus was the Messiah. They read the Scriptures and expected more of a political redeemer, one who would bring peace in the here and now. Others found his identification with God blasphemous. Others saw him as too dangerous a threat to the security of the nation. Finally, perhaps the most important reason: Jesus was a hard man to follow. There were the rigors of traveling with him, yes. But even more difficult was acting on his teachings. While the crowds loved him, as did some of the leaders, and they delighted in many of his teachings, his healings, and his quick mind, many of the Jewish leaders were less enamored of him. Jesus was a prophet. Prophets say hard things: he called out hypocrisy; he ruffled feathers; he disturbed the status quo. He wasn't cozy and cuddly. As things got more tense toward the end of his life, he called his students to "take up their cross." How's that for an end-of-life decision? Jesus didn't promise prosperity, ease, comfort, or acclaim. Instead, he drew a hard line in the sand. I think it would have taken an enormous amount of courage to follow him in those days. Perhaps for these reasons, he had more followers after his death than before.

Family Feud

Those who followed him before his death paid a price. Families were split by the decision of whether to follow Jesus: James and John followed Jesus. So did their mother. She even begged Jesus to give her boys important places in his ministry. But Zebedee, the brothers' father, stayed with the boats.[67] Joanna, the wife of Chuza, Herod's steward, followed Jesus; she even provided resources for Jesus and his ministry. But no word that Chuza ever did.[68] In light of this, I think Jesus' puzzling words begin to make more sense. "Do not suppose that I have come to bring peace to the earth. I did not come to bring peace, but a sword. For I have come to turn 'a man against his father, a daughter against her mother, a daughter-in-law against her mother-in-law—a man's enemies will be the members of his own household.' "[69]

But no matter how people responded to Jesus, it's important to remember that his entire life, death, resurrection, and ascension all happened within the context of the Jewish community. Over time, the church has looked at the life and times of Jesus from a religious, historical, and cultural distance. Once these stories of faith got printed, bound, and set inside churches, the Gospels lost their original context. It started to look like good guys versus bad guys, the faithful versus the faithless, Christians versus Jews, rather than Jesus standing with and for his own people. But in truth, there was no insider/outsider tension here. Rather, this was a family feud with intimate enemies. Pharisee, Sadducee, scribe, teacher of the Law, high priest, disciple, apostle, rabbi, teacher, sinner, tax collector, Jesus of Nazareth—these were all Jews. While they held diverse views, they shared more in common than not: Israel's covenant with God; the centrality of Torah; concern for the future and welfare of the Jewish people; the love of God.

Did the Jews reject Jesus? Certainly some did. They saw in him a provocative figure that flaunted Jewish practice and belief. To others he represented too dangerous a position for the stability of the nation. Still others did not see in him the realization of a Messiah. They chose different routes by which to be faithful to God and the people Israel.

Other Jews embraced him wholeheartedly. They formed the nucleus of Jesus' ministry—serving as disciples, apostles, patrons, protectors, and supporters. They risked their own lives to follow Jesus and to insure his message of the kingdom of God would be given a hearing and that his resurrection would be made known. They made a way for the Gentiles to follow Jesus as well. Without these courageous Jews, the ministry and message of Jesus would not be alive today. As Jesus himself said, "Salvation is from the Jews."[70]

4. Did the Jews Kill Jesus?

The Longest Hatred

I'm a big movie buff. But when *The Passion of the Christ,* Mel Gibson's controversial movie about the crucifixion of Jesus, came out on Ash Wednesday 2004, I decided against seeing it. I declined based on the violence and its potential anti-Jewish themes. I was in the minority in my circles; just about everyone else I knew flocked to see it.

One morning a few weeks after it came out, I sat in the coffee shop over breakfast with other pastors in my little Wyoming town. Talk turned to the movie and the role of Jews in Christ's death. "I don't know why Jews are saying this movie is anti-Semitic. After all, they <u>did</u> do it. The Scriptures say so," one Southern Baptist pastor flatly stated, shaking his head with a little laugh of disbelief.

His words hit me like a ton of bricks; how could he say that? Didn't he realize how statements like his have been used against the Jewish people for centuries? Didn't he know of the church's brutal history of anti-Semitism, called "the longest hatred"? Didn't he know about the trajectory of suffering words like his had launched, culminating in the Holocaust? He may not have known. If so, he wouldn't have been alone.

The vast majority of Christians, even well educated, are all but totally ignorant of what happened to Jews in history and of the culpable involvement of the Church. . . . It is little exaggeration to state that those pages of history Jews have committed to memory are the very ones that have been torn from Christian (and secular) history books.[1]

It's true. My childhood Sunday school classes focused not only on Bible lessons, Jewish holidays (several of which, including Purim, Passover, and Chanukah, are about surviving persecution), learning about other religions, but also anti-Semitism. We watched films on the Holocaust, which although not a Christian phenomenon, was made possible by centuries of Christian anti-Semitism. More on this in a bit. The year I was confirmed, our class went to Israel to experience our ancient homeland. When my older brothers were confirmed, their class trips took them to visit the Anne Frank house in Holland.

In case this history of anti-Semitism is new to you, I provide here a very brief recap: They tried to kill us. We survived. Let's eat! In the face of a very long history of persecution, Jewish survival has depended, in part, on a cultivating a resilient sense of humor.[2]

On a more somber note, here are some details to help you understand why the question "Did the Jews kill Jesus?" is so important. While the language of the New Testament has been called inherently anti-Semitic, with language like "His blood be on us and on our children,"[3] cited as proof positive that the Jews should suffer, the use of negative language about Jews increased over the centuries. As early as the second century, Christians charged Jews with deicide, or the murder of God. Here are the words of Bishop Melito of Sardis in an Easter sermon.

> Pay attention, oh families of the earth, and observe. An extraordinary murder has taken place in the center of Jerusalem, in the city devoted to God's Law, in the city of the Hebrews, in the city of the Prophets, in the city thought of as just. And who has been murdered? And who is the murderer? . . . God has been murdered. The king of Israel has been destroyed by the right hand of Israel."[4]

New Testament scholar Bart Ehrman suggests "this is the first time that any Christian charges Jews not just with the death of Jesus, but with the death of God."[5] But it wouldn't be the last. A whole genre of Jew-hate speech emerged, fanned by the flames of preachers, churchmen, and saints.

St. John Chrysostom, a fourth-century church father, whose name means "golden-mouthed," codified it in an eight-part sermon series called *Adversos Judaeos* (against the Jews). His preaching gave rise to the unofficial church doctrine known as contempt of the Jews.

> The synagogue is worse than a brothel...it is the den of scoundrels and the repair of wild beasts...the temple of demons devoted to idolatrous cults...the refuge of brigands and debauchees, and the cavern of devils. [It is] a criminal assembly of Jews...a place of meeting for the assassins of Christ...a house worse than a drinking shop...a den of thieves; a house of ill fame, a dwelling of iniquity, the refuge of devils, a gulf and abyss of perdition.[6]

Even though both Jewish and Christian scholars now think this sort of over-the-top language was a sign that Jews and Christians were still deeply tied and interconnected (a la "me thinks thou doth protest too much"), these words had a damning effect on Jews.

In the same century as the church consolidated its doctrines and power, Emperor Constantine enacted laws that isolated Jews both economically and socially. Physical violence against Jews accompanied these laws. Conversion to Judaism became a crime. Bringing Jews back to the fold from Christianity was punishable by death.[7] Officially, the policy of the church "was to allow small Jewish communities to survive in conditions of degradation and impotence." These humiliations were designed to demonstrate the triumph of church over synagogue.[8]

From this time into the Middle Ages, Jewish rights were systematically curtailed by European church councils, even as social and economic pressures continued. Here is but a sampling of edicts they issued: Jews must not appear in public during Holy Week, Jews seeking public office must be baptized, Jewish children are to be raised by Christians, Jews must pay tithes to support the church, no new synagogues may be built, ghettoes are compulsory for Jews. These church councils also prohibited Christians from observing the Sabbath, participating in Jewish holidays, and marrying Jews.[9]

Conditions worsened considerably over time for Jews in Christian lands. During the Crusades to protect the Holy Land, thousands of Jews were subject to the decision: convert or die. Often even when they did convert, they were later killed. At the close of the first Crusade in 1099, all the Jews living in Jerusalem were gathered into a synagogue and burned alive.[10] During the Spanish Inquisition, Jews who had converted—often under duress—were tortured to see if they would still profess the truth of Christianity.[11]

Finally, in 1492, the same year Columbus sailed the ocean blue, all Jews were expelled from Spain. But this wasn't the first time Jews were sent packing.[12] Beginning in 1290, Jews were expelled from every European society in which they lived—England, France, Hungary, Austria, Germany, Lithuania, Portugal, Bohemia, Moravia, and Russia.[13] In the thirteenth century, Jews were forced to wear special clothing to set them apart.[14] "Virtually all the Nuremburg laws were secularized and racist versions of prior Christian laws."[15]

Most pernicious of all was Martin Luther's sixteenth-century "advice" on how to deal with the "devilish" Jews—including burning their synagogues and their holy books, destroying their homes, forbidding rabbis to teach, stealing their gold, taking away their means of livelihood, and subjecting them to harsh labor. "This is to be done in honor of our Lord and of Christendom, so that God might see that we are Christians."[16] Clearly, he was unfamiliar with the song "They Will Know We Are Christians by Our Love"!

Four centuries later, Hitler enacted Luther's "advice" almost to the letter, resulting in the unspeakable evils of the Holocaust and the loss of vibrant European Jewry. Meanwhile much of the church looked the other way.[17] Raul Hillberg, scholar of the Holocaust sums up the Jewish position in society:

> Since the fourth century after Christ, there have been three anti-Jewish policies: [forced] conversion, expulsion, and annihilation. The second appeared as an alternative to the first, and the third emerged as an alternative to the second....The missionaries of Christianity had said in effect: You have no right to live among us as Jews. The secular rulers who followed proclaimed: You have no right to live among us. The Nazis at last decreed: You have no right to live.[18]

Jew hate speech didn't end there. It took on new forms such as the burning crosses of the Ku Klux Klan, swastikas desecrating synagogues, and strangely, Holocaust denial. Not to mention, among some circles, a push to question Israel's right to exist. Even now as anti-Semitism has greatly declined in the US, it is on the rise in Europe.[19]

Given this long history of hatred, no wonder so many of us were nervous about Mel Gibson's *The Passion of the Christ*. Would it spark an incendiary revival of anti-Semitism? Thankfully, that's not what happened. I am not proud to say, however, that in response to that pastor's assertion, I was mute. I didn't trust that I could say anything that would change his mind or his perception of the Scriptures, so I said nothing. Even so, I railed against him, silently, painfully aware of the consequences attitudes like his and muteness like mine have had on the Jewish people. It was certainly one of those days that I again wondered what a nice Jewish girl like me was doing in a place like this.

I've had more time to think since that day in 2004. Since I left local church ministry to write and teach, I've given dozens of presentations in churches on the Jewishness of Jesus, led Christian pilgrims to the Holy Land, and conducted many a Passover Seder in churches. I've learned a lot that I didn't know before.

Good Friday/Bad Friday

If there's one topic above all else that leaves both Jews and Christians feeling victimized, it's the death of Jesus. Not until last year did I have the courage to tackle the death of Jesus from a Jewish perspective. One Christian man voiced what others in my class were feeling one evening when he said, dark hurt in his eyes, "I just don't understand. How could *they* have killed *our* Messiah?"

Jews, on the other hand, still bear the psychic scars of centuries of actual victimization. Rabbi Lawrence Kushner articulated the feeling well:

> Somehow through the ages the suffering of Jesus has become confused with the suffering of the Jewish people, my people, me.... His death has even become causally linked with some denial on *my* part. And this in turn has been used as a justification for *my* suffering.
>
> In this way Jesus means for me—not the one who suffered for the world's sins—(sic) but the one *on account of whom* I must suffer.[20]

Remember the scene from the movie *Fiddler on the Roof* in which the wedding was violently disrupted by a group of Russians? Broken bottles, wounded people, and a wrecked party ensued. This riot or *pogrom* wasn't an isolated incident. Beginning with the first Crusade in the eleventh century and continuing up to the twentieth century, *pogroms* left thousands of Jews dead. Especially during Holy Week. Why Holy Week? "For almost 2,000 years in Western civilization, four words legitimized, rationalized, and fueled anti-Semitism: 'The Jews killed Christ,'" according to Abraham Foxman, national director of the Anti-Defamation League.[21] Church reenactments of the Passion, supported by fiery preaching, led inflamed Christians to seek revenge on Jews for deicide. Hitler capitalized on this when he "praised the Passion Play at Oberammergau, which dates back to 1633, saying that it was 'vital that it be continued...for never has the menace of Jewry been so convincingly portrayed as in this presentation of what happened in the times of the Romans.' "[22] I remember when some Christian friends excitedly invited me to join them on a pilgrimage to Oberammergau to see the Passion Play. Did I want to join them? Uh...no, thanks.[23]

It's time to ask: Did the Jews killed Jesus? That's easy to answer: no. The Gospels themselves are clear that Rome crucified Jesus. However, a different question, "Did the Jews have anything to do with killing Jesus?" nets a different response: it's complicated.

It's Complicated

Facebook has ten options for indicating your relationship status online. Here they are: single, in a relationship, engaged, married, divorced, in an open relationship, widowed, separated, in a domestic partnership, or in a civil union. That's a lot of choices. But if none of these quite fit, there's one more option you can check: It's complicated. Maybe he's not officially divorced or she's not officially single. Or perhaps the object of your love is clueless about your feelings. It's a handy term that applies to ambiguous situations.

"It's complicated" is also a fitting response for the question "Did the Jews have anything to do with killing Jesus?" The Bible offers four major explanations for the death of Jesus. First, Jesus gave himself up for us, knowingly and willingly. Second, his death was in accordance with God's will. Third, he was crucified by Rome. Fourth, ultimately it was "the Jews" who wanted him dead.

Why so many explanations? Consider this. The death of Jesus was unexpected. In retrospect, it seems like it was inevitable. But at the time it didn't. Whenever Jesus mentions his impending death in real time, the disciples are angry, confused, or upset. Peter even rebukes him saying, "God forbid it, Lord! This must never happen to you."[24] His heartfelt words speak for many. Such an ignominious death seemed inconceivable for the Son of God, the Messiah. It just didn't fit.

Jesus' death then raised troubling questions for his survivors. Had his followers made a mistake? Would they survive? Should they survive? What did his death say about God's relationship with Jesus? About the kingdom of God? Why didn't God protect him? The Gospels themselves are an attempt to explain the inexplicable. According to biblical scholar John Dominic Crossan, they were written to answer the question, "Why did Jesus die?"[25]

Even though his followers had immediate questions, it took decades for the answers to take shape. Doubtless, the answers arose as his followers discussed, prayed, and thought about all that happened and what it might mean. Those answers are the Gospels—written in different communities by different people, using different sources, at different times. They don't agree on everything. Not surprisingly, they contain a variety of stories, parables, references, themes, world views, assumptions, and even characterizations of the personality of Jesus. Some of which are at odds with each other. Like I said, it's complicated.

The First Jewish-Roman War

Complicating it even more, the Gospels were written in the midst of or in the aftermath of the First Jewish-Roman War, which took place during the years A.D. 66–73.[26] Mark, the earliest written Gospel, was likely written sometime between A.D. 65–75, Matthew sometime between A.D. 75 and 100. The exact dates of the composition of Luke and John are uncertain.[27]

The First Jewish-Roman War, which was the first of three Jewish uprisings against Roman occupation, changed everything. While tension with Rome had been building during Jesus' lifetime, it came to an explosive and destructive head just a few decades later. The Temple itself came under attack and was destroyed by the Romans in A.D. 70. First conceived of by King David and built by his son King Solomon as a permanent home for the ark of covenant, which had been housed by the tabernacle in the wilderness wanderings, it was later rebuilt by King Darius after the Jews returned from Babylonian exile. Finally the Temple was renovated by Herod the Great around 20 B.C. All told, the Temple stood in Jerusalem for the better part of one thousand years.[28]

Ancient and venerable, the Temple was central to Jewish identity. Remember, there was no concept of the separation of church and state in that era. The Temple formed the centerpiece of Jewish life—encompassing religion, governance, economics, community, and daily living. During the First Jewish-Roman War, Rome burned the Temple to the ground. It was utterly destroyed. Along with it, a way of life centuries in the making. Sacrifice—the form of Jewish worship for centuries—came to a sudden and screeching halt. The Holy of Holies—the sacred place where the divine presence dwelt and the high priest once a year sought repentance on behalf of all the people—was obliterated. The thrice yearly pilgrimages to Jerusalem—Passover, Feast of Weeks/Pentecost/Shavuot, and Feast of Booths/Sukkot to Feast of Booths—were no longer. Many of the Torah commands could not be carried out. All of this spelled a staggering loss to the Jewish nation. Marked now by an annual fast day (*Tisha B'Av*), all that's left of the site is the Western or Wailing Wall. The Dome of the Rock, a Muslim holy site, now sits atop or in close proximity to where the ancient Temple once stood.

Necessity is the mother of invention. Once the dust settled, Judaism eventually reinvented itself. Led by the rabbis or sages, spiritual successors to the Pharisees, synagogues became the new centers of community life. Piety, prayer, and study replaced sacrifice. The home became the new center of religious ritual. The oral law was written down in the form of the Mishnah and the Talmud. The party of the Sadducees disappeared from the Jewish landscape, and priests took on new sacred roles in synagogues. Rabbinic Judaism, as it has come to be called, is the forerunner of the types of Judaism practiced today.

The destruction of the Temple and Jerusalem also shaped the community of Jews who followed Rabbi Jesus. The universal peace and justice promised by the Messiah and the redemption of the Jewish people had not come to pass; Jerusalem lay in ruins. At the same time, more and more Gentiles were joining their ranks, further straining relations between the followers of Jesus and the larger Jewish community. Their response? The Gospels.

It's important to remember that the Gospels, and the New Testament as a whole, reflect intra-Jewish conflict. The unfolding story of Jesus in the Gospels is not a question of Jews versus Christians or Christians versus Jews. It's not even Jesus versus the Jewish people or the Jewish people versus Jesus. There is no "us versus them." These were Jews attempting to be faithful to God in the midst of tremendous social upheaval.

Four Explanations

With that historical background in mind, let's look more closely at the four explanations given by the Gospels for the death of Jesus. They are all deeply woven together, but I'll try to tease them apart.

1. Jesus offered himself knowingly and willingly.

How could a man as holy and powerful as Jesus wind up on a cross? Crucifixion was usually reserved for slaves, criminals, and others whom Rome used as an object lesson to demonstrate the consequences of bad behavior. Humiliating and excruciating (from the word *crucify*)—this form of capital punishment was known throughout the Empire for its brutality. What could explain this sort of death for Jesus? He must have given himself willingly. We see this idea expressed primarily in the Gospel of John. Jesus is depicted as moving purposefully, almost elegantly, toward the cross. When Jesus' soul is troubled, he is willing to face whatever is ahead of him so that he can glorify God.[29] He even asks as he is being arrested, "Am I not to drink the cup that the Father has given me?"[30] Jesus offers no defense when questioned. In Matthew, Mark, and Luke, he remains silent, while in John he deflects Pilate's questions. On the cross, Jesus utters his final words saying, "It is finished," before bowing his head and giving up his spirit.[31]

The other Gospels record Jesus urging his disciples, "If any want to become my followers, let them deny themselves and take up their cross and follow me."[32] That could mean only one thing: Jesus was willing to die and he wanted his disciples to be willing as well.

This idea of Jesus being a willing participant in his own death is captured in many Communion liturgies throughout Christendom. Before remembering how Jesus took and blessed bread and wine, we say these words: "On the night in which he gave himself up for us...." To this end, his self-sacrificing death served as atonement for humanity's sins and made salvation possible. But, according to the Gospel writers, Jesus didn't offer himself simply because he could see it was going to happen anyway. His death had God's stamp of approval on it.

2. Jesus died in accordance with the will of God.

When Peter rebukes Jesus for saying that he will be killed, Mark's Gospel hints at God's hand in it all. "Get behind me, Satan! For you are setting your mind not on divine things but on human things."[33] God is the invisible hand in all of this. In fact, the Gospels indicate that it was actually God's will that Jesus die. Jesus prays to God on the Mount of Olives: "Father, if you are willing, remove this cup from me; yet, not my will but yours be done."[34] It's hard to imagine that God's will for this beloved Son would be to die a horrible death. Certainly, no Messiah who would usher in peace and justice would die this kind of death. But this understanding might have been the only way for his followers to make sense of his death. Otherwise, why would Jesus have submitted to it? For that matter, how could God have allowed it to happen?

When Peter tries to fight against Jesus' arrest (in John's Gospel), Jesus stops him, saying, "Put your sword back in its sheath. Am I not to drink the cup the Father has given me?"[35] This isn't hopelessness Jesus is expressing; it expresses confidence in God's will.

We see Jesus' trust in God most clearly expressed in the Gospel of John. After questioning Jesus and finding no evidence against him, Pontius Pilate finally asks Jesus where he's from. Jesus is silent. He refuses to answer. Pilate goads him, "Do you not know that I have power to release you, and power to crucify you?" Jesus' confident response points to the power of God in the unfolding events. "You would have no power over me unless it had been given from above."[36]

3. The Romans did it.

Even as Jesus gives himself up willingly to the authorities in accordance with God's will, it is Pilate who condemns Jesus to death by crucifixion, the peculiarly Roman form of execution. Then Roman soldiers humiliate, mock, scorn, and beat Jesus before they hang him on the cross.

Rome would have its reasons to kill Jesus. Jesus' ministry revolved around the kingdom of God. He announced, proclaimed, taught about it, prayed for it, and taught others to do the same. If Jesus is ushering in a competing kingdom, and he's at its forefront, that's sedition.

Herod reacted with insane fear and violence when he heard a new king was born in Bethlehem. He went on a killing rampage reminiscent of Pharaoh's, murdering all the infants there. All in an attempt to wipe out the baby Jesus. When it came to killing, Herod, "perhaps the most vile human being ever to serve as a Jewish king,"[37] didn't stop with little babies. He killed members of his own family including his wife, three sons, and mother-in-law, fearful they might threaten his power. Now if

Herod killed his own relatives, who might or might not be pretenders to the throne, imagine how little sympathy Rome would have had for declared competition.

There's something to that because in each of the Passion stories, Pilate asks Jesus, "Are you the king of the Jews?" No matter that Jesus never says yes or no. He's turned over for crucifixion. Roman soldiers cruelly mock him by parroting homage to a king.

> Pilate . . . handed [Jesus] over to be crucified. Then the solders led him into the courtyard of the palace . . . clothed him in a purple cloak; and after twisting some thorns into a crown, they put it on him. And they began saluting him, "Hail King of the Jews!" They struck his head with a reed, spat upon him, and knelt down in homage to him. After mocking him, they stripped him of the purple cloak and put his own clothes on him. Then they led him out to crucify him. They compelled a passer-by . . . to carry his cross; . . . They brought Jesus to the place called Golgotha . . . offered him wine mixed with myrrh. . . . And they crucified him, and divided his clothes among them, casting lots to decide what each should take. It was nine o'clock in the morning when they crucified him.[38]

Finally, "The inscription of the charge against him read, 'The King of the Jews.' "[39] That he was hung with other criminals reinforces the idea that his was criminal behavior in the mind of Rome.

4. It was the Jews' fault.

Underneath all of this runs the theme of Jewish culpability for the death of Jesus. From the time some Pharisees and scribes began to seek and "plot" his death, to his arrest by Jewish authorities, to his questioning and trial by Jewish authorities, to the high priest turning him over to Pilate, to the vigorous accusations made by the chief priest and elders to Pilate, to the cries of "Crucify him!" from the crowd, to the people as a whole answering, "His blood be on us and our children!" the Gospels clearly express a significant Jewish role in Jesus' death.

Jesus rubs many Jewish leaders the wrong way. Perhaps his teaching was too radical. Perhaps others weren't ready for the kingdom of God. Perhaps his self-understanding—as Messiah, Son of God, one with the Father—offends the high priest as mocking God. Perhaps Jesus was a threat to national security. Or perhaps his in-your-face, prophetic announcements and cleansing of the Temple hit too close to home, threatening the powers that be.

Jesus came to Jerusalem at Passover just as the city was swelling with traveling Jewish pilgrims from all over Israel and the Diaspora. The large numbers of people in town combined with the fervent remembrance of freedom from slavery that Passover brings plus the presence of Roman occupation kindled a certain volatility. Feelings ran high. It was like a pot just about to boil; intense feelings simmered right below the surface.

In the midst of this tension, it wouldn't take much for Jesus or his followers to invoke a riot at Passover. Say, causing a disturbance in the Temple. Or cutting off the ear of a Roman slave. Both of which happened. That could put the whole Jewish population at risk. In fact, each year at the festival, troops were moved into Jerusalem to discourage an uprising. Rome wasn't afraid to use them either. Troublemakers were regularly put down at Passover, the Festival of Freedom.[40]

Caiaphas, appointed by Rome, "juggled the religious interests of Jews and the political interests of Rome, at whose pleasure [he] served."[41] This balancing spells trouble for Jesus after he raises Lazarus from the dead. The trouble Caiaphas notes is political, not theological.

> So the chief priests and the Pharisees called a meeting of the council, and said, "What are we to do? This man is performing many signs. If we let him go on like this, everyone will believe in him, and the Romans will come and destroy both our holy place and our nation."[42]

Written after the destruction of the holy Temple, the destruction of Jerusalem, and the dispersion of Israel, these fears expressed in the Gospel of John are real indeed.

> But one of them, Caiaphas, who was high priest that year, said to them, "You know nothing at all! You do not understand that it is better for you to have one man die for the people than to have the whole nation destroyed."[43]

Caiaphas's strategy was spot-on and terribly ironic: sacrifice one person for the good of all.

> He did not say this on his own, but being high priest that year he prophesied that Jesus was about to die for the nation, and not for the nation only, but to gather into one the dispersed children of God.[44]

Even as Israel was about to be dispersed, an increasing number of Gentiles were being drawn to belief in the God of Israel.

> So from that day they planned to put him to death.[45]

Citing both theological and political reasons, the Gospels fix responsibility for Jesus' death—with increasing pointedness from the earliest written Gospel, Mark, to the final Gospel, John—on Jewish leaders.

So, were the Jews to blame for Jesus' death? We have one more set of historical considerations to look at. Before we dive into those, let's review. First, Jesus was a Jew; these were all Jews involved in a Jewish movement. Second, Jesus' death was unexpected, shocking his followers. Third, it took them time to shape the answers to the questions it raised. By the time the Gospels were written, Jerusalem had fallen, the Temple had been destroyed, and the two communities were beginning to diverge. The social context in which the authors of the Gospels wrote was very different than the one encountered by Jesus' Jewish followers. Fourth, the Gospels give major answers for why Jesus died, reflecting the ambiguity his followers felt about his death. Fifth, Jewish culpability is but one thread in the Gospels; yet it has been used with singular violence against Jews, making an otherwise good and holy Friday into a bad Friday indeed.

Three Approaches to the Passion Narratives

As we have noted, in the past, the church has used the charge of deicide or murder of God as an opportunity to vilify, blame, and exact revenge on Jews. Thankfully that's changing. Vatican II, the 1962–1965 Council of the Roman Catholic Church that addressed itself to the modern world, absolved the Jewish people as a whole of killing Jesus. It recognized Judaism as an ongoing, living religion to be respected, rather than a sign of disobedience to God. It extended respect to Jews as ongoing participants in covenantal relationship with God rather than as unbelieving people needing to be converted or wiped out. Many Protestant denominations followed suit. Given these developments, it seems to me that there are three appropriate responses for the Christian.

Limited Liability

Saying "the Jews" killed Jesus is like saying all white people killed Martin Luther King, Jr. Preposterous! In fact, many whites marched with and supported King. Only a few were responsible. Isn't it the same thing with the Jews? Let "the Jews" off the hook and move on without rancor or blame.

Forgiveness

You could say, yes, some Jews killed Jesus—but he stands for love and forgiveness, and so do we. So we forgive them. Besides look how much good came out of it! We now have the forgiveness of sins, the resurrection of Jesus, and salvation for all people. I've often wondered, if it was God's will that Jesus die for the sins of humanity, then why cast aspersions on Jews at all? Why blame? Doesn't it make more sense to give quiet thanks that God's plan was accomplished?

What Is Truth?

As Jews and Christians have engaged in dialogue, brokered reconciliation, and studied anew each other's histories, religions, and sacred texts, a third response is gaining attention. In a dramatic moment, before turning Jesus over for crucifixion, Pilate speaks with Jesus, asking him, "What is truth?"[46] In the same way, we can ask: Are these Passion stories historically accurate? I realize this question represents a challenge. Faith is after all a matter of, well, faith. Does historical accuracy really matter? And can we even know?

Many texts are taken on faith and mined for the spiritual principles they embody. It matters little if they actually happened exactly that way or not. They are metaphors for larger spiritual truths. Were Adam and Eve the first two human beings? Was Jonah swallowed by a whale? Did the Red Sea split in two? Does it actually matter? But in this case, where the charge of Christ-killers against "the Jews" has led to such murderous results, I think it does matter.

Some faith perspectives won't allow for this type of questioning at all. Others, like United Methodism, not only allow for it but welcome it. Scripture, experience, tradition, and reason are the four sources by which one comes to and confirms his or her faith. The quadrilateral, as these four sources are called, is one of the chief reasons I chose to be ordained in this denomination. Or maybe it chose me! It's a holistic approach that includes heart and head, past and present. It engages the fullness of one's being for the spiritual journey. Permission to use one's heart and head doesn't mean we will all arrive at the same conclusion. Far from it! People of deep faith and solid learning can and do conscientiously disagree. But if you're game, let's take a closer look at some of the historical elements in question.

First, a caveat. I'm no expert on these historical matters. Scholars who tread these waters read the sources in their original languages, are well versed in the principles of historical inquiry, and understand the ins and outs of ancient texts and ancient history. As for me, I learned basic Hebrew in Hebrew school, chanted from the Torah and Prophets at my bat mitzvah, learned more about Torah, Mishnah, and Talmud as a Jewish adult, and aced my seminary courses in Hebrew, Greek, Old Testament, and New Testament. It's made my mom proud. But an expert I'm not. Still, I am deeply curious about these things and have read with great interest what Jewish and Christian scholars are saying. That's what I'd like to share with you here. I'll be drawing heavily on several works including *The Jewish Annotated New Testament*, edited by Jewish New Testament scholars, Amy-Jill Levine and Marc Zvi Brettler. Let's take a closer look, shall we?

Timing of the Trial

They took Jesus to the high priest; and all the chief priests, the elders, and the scribes were assembled.[47]

First, the timing of the trial is doubtful. By the time they took Jesus to the high priest, it was late on the first night of Passover. Remember, they had already eaten the Passover meal, sung a hymn, gone to Gethsemane to pray where the disciples were too sleepy to stay awake, and then gone through an arrest. That means a trial would have started quite late on this very holy night. Or even in the early hours of the next day. But according to the Mishnah—a book of Jewish learning and law—activities like this would be strictly forbidden. All work like this would have had to stop by noon of that day. That Jewish law mattered greatly is affirmed by the fact that the women didn't go to Jesus' tomb right after he was taken down from the cross. They waited almost two days until after the Sabbath was over to prepare Jesus for burial.

Testimony

For many gave false testimony against him, and their testimony did not agree. Some stood up and gave false testimony against him, saying, "We heard him say, 'I will destroy this temple that is made with hands, and in three days I will build another, not made with hands.' " But even on this point their testimony did not agree. Then the high priest stood up before them and asked Jesus, "Have you no answer? What is it that they testify against you?" But he was silent and did not answer.[48]

At the trial of Jesus, false and conflicting testimony is given. Biblically, testimony from two witnesses is required for any kind of conviction.[49] Bearing false witness, one of the "you shall nots" in the Ten Commandments, is absolutely unlawful.[50] In my mind, for a people of the Law to disregard its own laws to convict a man accused of breaking the law also puts this part of the trial in question. All in all, twenty-seven breaches of Jewish law have been noted in these proceedings.[51] Perhaps Jesus was such a threat that they felt it was worth turning over time-honored Jewish law and bypassing well-documented criminal procedures to silence him. That may be. The next point however is where things get really interesting.

Barabbas and "Custom"

There is one last out for Jesus before being marched to the cross. And that is to let another man die in his stead. Pilate offers, in all four Gospels, to release Jesus and to hold or execute a man named Barabbas instead.

Now at the festival [Pilate] used to release a prisoner for them, anyone for whom they asked. Now a man called Barabbas was in prison with the rebels who had committed murder during the insurrection. So the crowd came and began to ask Pilate to do for them according to his custom. Then he answered them, "Do you want me to release for you the King of the Jews?" For he realized that it was out of jealousy that the chief priests had handed him over. But the chief priests stirred up the crowd to have him release Barabbas for them instead. Pilate spoke to them again, "Then what do you wish me to do with the man you call the King of the Jews?" They shouted back, "Crucify him!" Pilate asked them, "Why, what evil has he done?" But they shouted all the more, "Crucify him!" So Pilate, wishing to satisfy the crowd, released Barabbas for them; and after flogging Jesus, he handed him over to be crucified.[52]

Several things are interesting here. After scouring ancient documents—both Jewish and Roman—scholars find no historical evidence for the custom of releasing a prisoner at the festival. On the contrary, Rome had a practice of silencing seditionists and quashing insurrectionaries at the festival. Passover was the toughest time of year for them to keep the peace. Extra troops were brought in to quell riots. It seems highly unlikely that they would release Barabbas, a rebel and murderer at just this time of year.

Little detail is given about Barabbas. Dig into the meaning of his name, though, and it has quite a bit to tell us. *Barabbas* is Aramaic for "son of the father." As twentieth-century scholars point out, "'Son of the Father' is the title which belongs to Jesus in a completely special and transcendental way."[53] To cloud things even more, Barabbas is also known as Jesus Barabbas in some texts. So here we have before us two men known as Son of the Father. Which one should be let go? Jesus of Nazareth, who was brought on trumped-up charges in an illegal proceeding, or Barabbas, the notorious criminal? The crowd calls for the notorious criminal to be let go, and the miracle-working, prophet-rabbi to be crucified. I've always thought that was unlikely. Especially given that, less than a week earlier, Jesus was cheered and hailed as he entered Jerusalem on a donkey and that throughout his ministry the crowds supported him.

The scholars weigh in. Levine and Brettler's volume suggests that "Barabbas is . . . likely an invented double for Jesus."[54] Others say the whole thing is the stuff of legendary fiction.

> That the people, in front of captive Jesus, passed suddenly from admiration to hatred and that, to not contentedly . . . prefer Barabbas to him, they asked with rage that Pilate crucify him; that Pilate lent himself at once to this furious whim. Those are all details, which fit better the category of legendary fiction than history and which would rather resemble for a purpose of theater in a melodrama or a childish tale rather than with reality.[55]

If Barabbas is an invented double for Jesus, what does that say about the role and character of Pilate?

Pilate

In the Gospels, Pilate appears to be a sensitive even merciful person. He figures out the underlying motives of Jesus' accusers—jealousy; tries to save an innocent man—Jesus; but in the end bends to the will of the crowd—crucify him!—while washing his hands of innocent blood. He seems to be a decent man. Independent historical sources of the day, however, such as the Jewish historians Josephus and Philo as well as the Roman historian Tacitus, reflect Pilate in a very different light.

Concerning Jesus' executioner, Pontius Pilate, we have a considerable body of data that contradicts the largely sympathetic portrayal of him in the New Testament. Even among the long line of cruel procurators who ruled Judea, Pilate stood out as a notoriously vicious man. He eventually was replaced after murdering a group of Samaritans: The Romans realized that keeping him in power would only provoke continual rebellions. The gentle, kindhearted Pilate of the New Testament—who in his "heart of hearts" really did not want to harm Jesus is fictional. Like most fictions, the story was created with a purpose. When the New Testament was written, Christianity was banned by Roman law. The Romans, well aware that they had executed Christianity's founder—indeed the reference to Jesus' crucifixion by the Roman historian Tacitus is among the earliest allusions to him outside the New Testament—had no reason to rescind their anti-Christian legislation. Christianity's only hope for gaining legitimacy was to "prove" to Rome that its crucifixion of Jesus had been a terrible error, and had only come about because the Jews forced Pilate to do it. Thus, the New Testament depicts Pilate as wishing to spare Jesus from punishment, only to be stymied by a large Jewish mob yelling, "Crucify him." The account ignores one simple fact. Pilate's power in Judea was absolute. Had he wanted to absolve Jesus, he would have done so: He certainly would not have allowed a mob of Jews, whom he detested, to force him into killing someone whom he admired.[56]

Although independent historical records reveal Pilate as a cruel leader who unnecessarily provoked the people under his rule, the church remembers him differently.

After the dissemination of the Gospels, Pilate was even considered a convert to Christianity, and he is honored as a martyr in the Coptic

Orthodox Church; his feast day is June 25. The transfer of guilt from the Romans—who crucified Jesus—to the Jews was then complete.[57]

Finally, let's look more closely at crucifixion itself.

Crucifixion

Crucifixion was a cruel and prolonged form of execution; a form of "public terrorism" Rome used against slaves, criminals, and dissenters as a deterrent against bad behavior. That Jesus was crucified makes it clear that he was executed for offenses under Roman, not Jewish law. Rabbi Telushkin reports this:

> Crucifixion…was forbidden by Jewish law because it was torture. Some 50,000 to 100,000 Jews were themselves crucified by the Romans in the first century. How ironic, therefore, that Jews have historically been associated with the cross as the ones who brought about Jesus' crucifixion.[58]

Well, Did the Jews Kill Jesus?

We've covered a lot of history here. And we get back to the question we started with. Did the Jews kill Jesus? No. Romans executed him by crucifixion for the crime of sedition. Did Jewish leaders play a part? The Gospel writers insist they did. On the other hand, biblical historians cast doubt on the veracity of passages that most strongly implicate them. Their findings suggest a much more muted role of the Jewish leaders. Bottom line: it's complicated. We'll never know for sure. But this we can know. The suffering, death, and resurrection of Jesus is absolutely vital to Christians. He died for the sins of the world. His saving death has brought love, hope, and forgiveness to billions of people worldwide. Here's where I stand: holding this event sacred while treating it with sensitivity is important for keeping love alive while letting anti-Semitism die.

The Times They Are a-Changin'

Earlier I said the death of Jesus was one of the most divisive points between Christians and Jews. The good news, as we preachers like to say, is that since Vatican II, Christians and Jews have been engaged in the most productive and fervent interfaith dialogue ever. Once the charge of deicide was officially dropped from liturgy by the Roman Catholic Church, and with it the charge of perpetual guilt, tensions have greatly declined. This has opened the way for Christians and Jews to see each other anew.

Not only have Christians and Jews been engaged in fruitful dialogue, but…wait for it…Jews have engaged Jesus in turn! I'm not talking about mass conversions here. Although I've discovered I'm not the only Jew Jesus has appeared to; not by a long shot. Rather, I'm talking about Jews taking an honest assessment of the Jewish Jesus. This is happening in scholarly, academic, and congregational life. It's truly amazing; fifty-five years ago this would have been unheard of.

Not that everyone is in agreement. Nevertheless, for centuries, Jesus' name was not even to be uttered by Jews, so associated with it was our suffering. That was true even when I was growing up. This too is changing dramatically.

My favorite sign of this shift is the title of a dog-eared book I own, *Jesus through Jewish Eyes: Rabbis and Scholars Engage an Ancient Brother in a New Conversation.*[59] Beyond volumes like this, there are a rapidly growing number of Jewish New Testament professors in both Jewish and Christian colleges and seminaries. Christian scholars, teachers, and preachers draw upon Jewish insights. Scores of organizations and websites are devoted to offering insight into the Jewish roots of Christianity. The times they are a-changin'. I can't help but think all of this is helping to contribute to a more peaceful world. Thanks be to God!

5. Has God
Rejected the Jews?

Jerusalem (SatireWire.com) Update—Jews, whose troubled, 10,000-year term as God's "chosen people" finally expired last night, woke up this morning to find that they had once again been hand-picked by the Almighty. Synagogues across the globe declared a day of mourning.

Asked if the descendants of Abraham shouldn't be pleased about being tapped for an unprecedented second term, Jerusalem Rabbi Ben Meyerson shrugged. "Of course, you are right, we should be thrilled," he said. "We should also enjoy a good swift kick in the head, but for some reason, we don't.

"Now don't ask such questions until you watch the news, or read history, or at least rent *Fiddler on the Roof*.[1]

Can't You Choose Someone Else?

I know just about every song from *Fiddler on the Roof* by heart. Much of the dialogue too. The record album was practically sacramental in our household growing up. We played it again and again, trying to match Tevye in singing "If I Were a Rich Man" and dancing joyously around the house. It touched something deep in us, although it pointed to a Jewish experience we knew only vicariously. Still, there were pieces we could directly relate to. One day Tevye talks to God about being chosen. "I know, I know. We are Your chosen people. But, once in a while, can't You choose someone else?" Cue the laughter. You'd think that being "chosen" would somehow feel better!

To be sure, life in our New England town was quite different from nineteenth-century Eastern Europe. There were no pogroms, no Jewish ghettos, no comparison. Thank God! Still, being chosen didn't always feel so good for us either. My brothers, sister, and I were one of two or three Jewish kids in our respective classrooms. Throughout my grade school years I definitely had the sense of being different and felt the need to hide or protect myself in order stay safe. Sure, there was the usual name-calling most kids endured. Some of it related to wearing glasses: "four eyes"; and some to being an early bloomer: "Charmin," as in "squeezably soft." I could have lived without all of that. But most painful of all was the name calling related to being Jewish, "Jew, kike, yid." It made me acutely aware of being in the minority and the vulnerability that brings.

My parents experienced it too. My Catholic father, born to a Polish mother and an Italian father, endured pressure for years from seemingly well-meaning evangelical Christians—both because he wasn't Protestant and because he and my Jewish mom were "intermarried." Interestingly, my mom was the daughter of a Reform Jewish mother and an Orthodox father. In her parents' day, their marriage was also considered "intermarriage." Anyway, my dad was quick to remind us kids that we weren't WASP's. Now that I think about it, I realize he may have been focused on the Anglo-Saxon Protestant part. But I figured he meant we weren't white either. I guess it stuck. I still resist being referred to as white. Maybe that has to do with the awareness of Hitler's Aryan "race," too.

It wasn't until my college graduation trip to Israel with my grandmother when I was twenty-four that I finally experienced the carefree feeling of being in the majority. Surrounded by other Jews, fear and guardedness fell away, shrugged off like a coat in warm weather—simply unnecessary. With a sigh of relief, I melted into the multihued, multilingual, diverse society I found there. To be sure, there are distinctions in Israeli society based on one's degree of religiosity. The size and shape of male head coverings carries a whole calculus of meaning. Round fur hats, small knit yarmulkes, and 1940s style hats each carry a coded message about the kind of Jew who wears it and the norms of their religious observance. I think I was too relieved to notice any of that at the time. I simply drank in the fact that being Jewish was acceptable.

I sensed a similar ease when I first walked into Scott United Methodist Church, some eight years later, joining the well-dressed stream of African Americans who entered the church for Sunday morning worship. Although I wasn't black, I got what it was to move from minority to majority status simply by walking into a building. It was a move from "other" to "us," from being an object of suspicion to being an honored individual, from feeling guarded to breathing easily. It was an interesting juxtaposition to be in the minority among minorities. Somehow it increased my sense of safety.

When the position of associate pastor was created at Scott UMC a few years later, I became the first non-black clergyperson to serve the church there as well as their first female minister and the first Jewish Christian most of them knew. I introduced them to the intersection of Jewish, Christian, and black experience in the Bible. They schooled me in the joy, determination, and pain of the African-American experience. We had a lot in common. Those were glorious, heady years. When I left several years later to co-pastor another church, it was as a member of the family. Our shared experience of being "other" made all the difference.

Why does anti-Semitism exist? Why racism against blacks? Why prejudice of any sort? I wonder if it can't be traced to a skewed misunderstanding of chosenness. We belong and you don't. We're right and you're wrong. We're superior and you're inferior. I say *skewed* because this one up/one down orientation doesn't fit with the biblical notion of chosenness.

What Does It Mean to Be Chosen?

From a Jewish perspective, here's what *chosen* doesn't mean. Chosen doesn't mean Jews, upon death, are routed up to heaven while everyone else is funneled down into hell. Heaven and hell as popularly understood now aren't categories in the traditional Jewish psyche; Judaism concerns itself primarily with the here and now. Chosen doesn't mean Jews are chosen for eternal salvation while others are rejected. In Jewish thinking salvation means communal well-being, again, primarily in the here and now. But it also refers to the "coming age" when God's rule will be established on earth. At this time, all nations of the earth will be saved. It's a kind of universal salvation. By the way, do you hear echoes of the Lord's Prayer in this idea? Jesus was expressing deeply Jewish sentiments when he taught the disciples to pray, "Your kingdom come, Your will be done, on earth as it is in heaven." Chosen also doesn't mean Jews are the only ones loved by God. Or that Jews are the only ones approved by God. Judaism teaches that all humans are created in the image and likeness of God. In fact, we all—Jew and Gentile—bear the image of God within us. Judaism doesn't even teach the concept of original sin or a fallen creation; that idea gained prominence with Augustine in the fourth century.[2]

Chosen doesn't mean Jews are superior to anyone else—whether racially, ethnically, spiritually, historically, intellectually, or economically. Certainly not athletically—although we gladly lay claim to Sandy Koufax, Hank Greenberg, and the pro basketball team in Tel Aviv. As Moses reminded the Israelites, there wasn't anything special about them as a people when God chose them for covenant relationship. They weren't chosen based on their merit but on God's grace.[3] Finally, chosen definitely doesn't mean that Jews are divinely targeted for suffering or punishment. I well remember the day someone whom I thought should know better offered up an "insight" in a DISCIPLE Bible Study class that the Holocaust was God's punishment of the Jews for not following Jesus. Unlike Tevye, he wasn't kidding about divine punishment. I had to count to ten through clenched teeth before I could respond to him. So what does being chosen mean?

The concept starts with the call of God to Abraham to leave behind all that he knew and set out on a journey to a new land. According to Jewish *midrash* (stories that explain and expand the values, themes, and stories in the Bible), Abraham's father made and sold idols. Once when he was young, and left alone in his father's shop, Abram (as he was known then) smashed all the idols and put the hammer in the hands of another idol. When his father returned, he saw all his workmanship destroyed and demanded to know what happened. Abram told his father that the idol had done it. His father knew better; he knew that couldn't have been the case since the idol wasn't alive but made out of stone. In that moment, Abram's point was made about the futility of idol worship.[4]

When Abram set out on the road trip that would establish monotheism and usher in Judaism, he was already a believer in one God. As the first Jew he received the first covenantal promise made by God to the Jewish people:

> I will make of you a great nation, and I will bless you, and make your name great, so that you will be a blessing. I will bless those who bless you, and the one who curses you I will curse; and in you all the families of the earth shall be blessed.[5]

The promises didn't end there. God promises Abram that his descendants will be as numerous as the stars in the sky,[6] that he'll be the "ancestor of a multitude of nations,"[7] and that he and his offspring will possess the land "for a perpetual holding."[8] Note these promises aren't stamped with an expiration date. They're not conditional. They're everlasting; good in perpetuity.[9] Recognized through the deliverance from slavery, set in stone tablets at Mount Sinai, enacted in the long desert trek of the Israelites with the pillar of cloud by day and the pillar of fire by night, referenced by the prophets who called the people back to it, this covenantal relationship took on increasing depth and meaning throughout the Bible. Again and again it is affirmed in Scripture: "I will be your God and you will be my people."[10]

Sure there are prejudiced, chauvinistic Jews who interpret chosenness in ways exactly opposite of what I am discussing. Likewise, there Jews who are so assimilated that the idea of being chosen has no meaning at all for them. But for the most part, here is what chosenness does mean to us: to be in covenantal relationship with God. It means serving God and bringing the world to the knowledge of this one God. Finally, it means living in such a way that the world is perfected under the rule of God; its brokenness repaired *(tikkun olam)*.

You may be thinking this all sounds very Christian. In a way, it does. That's because Christians, like Jews, understand themselves to be called to act as "a light unto the nations." Great, I say! The more light the better. It seems to me that it will take all of us to repair the brokenness in this world. Others agree. As one Jewish prayer book acknowledges,

> Israel gave birth in time to other religions that have brought many to God. But our responsibility continues, for our mission remains unfulfilled. It will continue until the earth is full of the knowledge of the Lord as the sea-bed is covered by water.[11]

Even as Jews claim their special mission in the world, many Jews today are embarrassed by the whole notion of chosenness. A lot of suffering has accompanied it. In fact, some Jewish denominations have dropped the idea altogether. You won't hear much talk about it in most

Jewish communities; it's even dropped out of some prayer books.[12] But not talking about it doesn't mean it isn't there. Chosenness is deeply woven into the Jewish psyche. Just as it is in the Christian psyche. While it's embedded in the words of the Hebrew Bible, it's formatted into the very structure of the Christian Bible. Open your Kindle or grab a Bible off the shelf, look at the table of contents, and you'll see what I mean. Christian Bibles are divided into two parts: the Old Testament, which is a rearranged version of the Hebrew Bible, and the New Testament. The word testament means "covenant." The implicit understanding is that the New Testament contains God's new covenant with all people; the Old Testament contains God's old covenant with the Jews. You can also hear it in the language of Communion: "This is the blood of the new covenant, which was poured out for you and for many." The word new doesn't actually appear in the accounts of the Last Supper in Matthew and Mark. It appears in Luke and First Corinthians, however.[13] Sometimes old means "older" or "first"; but here it generally means "outdated, no longer in force," or even "no longer necessary." The author of Hebrews says it is "obsolete and growing old."[14]

Has the Church Taken Israel's Place as the Chosen People?

The idea that God's covenant with the Jews is obsolete is called "supersessionism" or replacement theology. Here's how the thinking goes. Jesus first came to the Jews who rejected him. In rejecting Jesus, they rejected God. In turn, God has rejected the Jews and selected Christians to carry his message to the world. Christians have replaced or superseded Jews as the new Israel. Thus Christians are now the chosen people of God. The new covenant has replaced the old covenant. With Christianity as the sole inheritor of the promises to Israel, Judaism is deemed irrelevant, obsolete, dead. Thus, the question of this chapter: Has God rejected the Jews?

Put another way, has the church taken Israel's place as the chosen people? If so, there's just one tiny problem. God neglected to mention it to the Jews! Rather than die off as Christianity has taken off, Judaism has flourished through the ages. This fact is what so frustrated and intrigued church leaders over the centuries who saw themselves as the sole inheritors of the promises of Jeremiah 31:31: "The days are surely coming, says the Lord, when I will make a new covenant with the house of Israel and the house of Judah." Jeremiah goes on to prophesy that this covenant will be unlike the previous one made at Mount Sinai. Rather than being etched in stone, it will be inscribed directly on the human heart, placed directly in the human mind.[15] In keeping with a "freed from the Law" reading of Paul, Christians have historically seen this new covenant as Torah-less.

Written some 650 years before Hebrews, Jeremiah 31 meant something entirely different to the people who first heard and read it.

> In its original context, Jeremiah was suggesting that the Torah would be renewed after the Babylonian exile by being planted in people's hearts or minds, so they could instinctively observe it; therefore they won't any longer sin, and so there would not be another exile.[16]

When the passage was originally written, it was a comforting assurance of God's continuing relationship with the Jews. It wasn't a hint that they would one day be bumped.

To be fair, I don't know whether most Christians look at Judaism this way today: bumped, expired, obsolete. In fact, I doubt they do. This language of supersessionism may simply be part of the family feud dynamic we identified in Chapter 3. It's possible that Hebrews was even written by a Jewish Christian believer and preached in synagogues.[17] But the fact that it's now part of the Christian canon and read in churches gives Hebrews its supersessionist one-two punch. And it contributes to an us versus them mentality that keeps Jews and Christians suspicious of one another.

Make no mistake. There's nothing wrong with other faiths seeing themselves as having a special relationship with God. God is big enough to lovingly and purposefully engage all of humanity. If not, this is not a God with whom I want to be in relationship. I'm a big believer that every individual and every people group has a purpose. In the language of the black church, "God don't make no junk!" But isn't there a way to claim a special relationship with God without stamping out the other guy?

In essence, that's what Christian replacement theology does. It takes the Jewish Bible, with its concept of chosenness and, in a twist, turns it against Jewish people. Chosenness, which for Jews does not mean an exclusivistic love of God toward them, but rather an exacting responsibility toward God, now has an opposite if unintended meaning. In order to get in on God's covenantal love, Jews must first become Christian. If you follow Jesus you're in; if you follow Torah you're out. Out of covenant, that is. Plus, you're probably going to hell. This, by the way, from a tradition that claims a God of universal love!

Has God rejected the Jews? If biblical promises are to be trusted, no. Paul, too, affirms that God's gifts and call are irrevocable.[18] Seeing the error of its previous stance, the Vatican has weighed in on this too: "Although the Church is the new people of God, the Jews should not be presented as rejected or accursed by God, as if this followed from the Holy Scriptures."[19]

Supersessionism is one of the principles of Christianity I've always had a hard time swallowing. It just doesn't seem like a logical conclusion for a religion centered around a Jewish rabbi. To be sure, many Christians believe that since God is love, God truly does love all people, including Jews. And depending on who you ask, especially Jews. Even so, perhaps more than any other Christian tenet, replacement theology has compelled me to search for the Jewish roots of the Christian message, to see if perhaps something has gotten lost in the translation.

To finally settle this question, we have one more question to ask: Has God or God's envoy, the apostle Paul, rejected the Torah? If so, then we might as well say God has rejected the Jews. It's about the same thing. As we to turn our attention to the writings of Paul, we'll discover something altogether more wonderful, more inclusive, and perhaps to the modern mind, more scandalous.

Me and Paul

Typically, Paul has been seen by Christians as the first convert to Christianity. By Jews he's been seen as the ultimate apostate. Why? Not only did he leave his religion behind, but he seemed to declare it null and void, laying the foundation for supersessionism. With it, millennia of bad blood between Jews and Christians. I feel sorry for the guy. Can I be honest with you? This is the first time I've felt that way for Paul. I've had an uneasy relationship with him over the years. When given the chance to preach on the letters of Paul or the Gospels or the Hebrew Bible or even the Psalms, I almost always pass on Paul.

First off, I find him hard to understand. Can I get an "amen"? These aren't straightforward stories he tells, like other parts of the Bible, or even parables with hidden meanings. I'd take parables with hidden meanings over Paul, believe me. Rather, he writes letters in a technical, legal language that is hard to understand. Secondly, his pronouncements that do seem clear are harsh: women are solidly anchored as second-class citizens, equal rights for homosexual relationships are out of the question, slaves get no quarter from him, citizens must submit unquestioningly to political powers whether good or bad, and the Torah and those who follow it are trashed.

Let's take a closer look at Paul and the Torah. Not all of his statements line up with each other. Some of them are downright contradictory. On the one hand Paul writes that the Law is holy, just, good, and spiritual.[20] On the other hand, he says "Christ redeemed us from the curse of the law"[21] and "Now we are discharged from the law," no longer "slaves" to the old written code.[22] Which is it? Over the centuries, the church has tended to vote in favor of the latter, supporting the creation of a supposedly grace-filled, law-free, Torah-less church. But that position doesn't adequately make sense of all the positive things Paul says about Israel and the Law, such as Jews being entrusted with the oracles of God that did not fail.[23]

I remember when, as a seminary student, I mentioned in a Bible study that the Bible is contradictory in places. I got a smiling but pointed response from Mrs. Polk, the head prayer warrior at Scott United Methodist Church and eventually a dear friend, who told me that I simply wasn't reading deeply enough. I reserved judgment at the time. But Mrs. Polk, I have to agree with you on this one. That's because, thankfully, new readings of Paul are emerging that make more sense of his apparent contradictions. I have especially enjoyed reading N. T. Wright, Pamela Eisenbaum, and Mark Nanos.[24] The last two are Jewish New Testament scholars, of which there are a growing number. All three relocate Paul in his Jewish context. All three engage other Jewish writings of the time to help shed light on Paul's assumptions, language, world view, values, and beliefs. To great effect!

Okay, time for another confession. As much as I have loved Jesus, I have held a part of myself back from Christianity. Yes, I know I am an ordained minister. I know I have taken vows. The thing is, I'm good with Jesus. It's Christianity I have been suspicious of. You probably understand my wariness if you've gotten this far in the book. Much of it has had to do with what Paul has written. Or as I am coming to understand, the way he has been interpreted.

Along with John Wesley my heart is now being strangely warmed. Wesley's heart thawed when he heard Luther's introduction to Romans being read at a class meeting. My heart is thawing, fluttering, and opening as I read Eisenbaum and Nanos on Romans.

Romans contains Paul's most mature, nuanced position on Jesus, Jews, Gentiles, and the Law. From it Wesley received assurance of God's love that long ago night in Aldersgate. As for me, I am receiving insight that Paul was a deeply committed Jew fulfilling a uniquely Jewish vision in the world. I'm receiving assurance that my Judaism and my discipleship aren't so at odds with each other. A hidden dimension of unity exists. And it's revealed through this new way of reading Paul.[25] Strange, yes. Warm, definitely. It turns out God does know what God is doing in my life. These new readings of Paul are inspiring in me a larger vision of Christianity, a grander appreciation for Judaism, and a sense of personal peace that has long been missing in my spiritual journey. My thanks to these scholars from whose insights I have deeply drawn. They are reflected in the remainder of this chapter.

Reading Paul Again for the First Time

To set the stage for the new understandings of Paul, let's consider where we have been. Paul has long been read through the lens of Martin Luther who imagined Judaism as a religion of works-righteousness and Christianity as a religion of grace. In the first scenario, a person stacks up credits to convince God that their merits outweigh their demerits; God obliges with salvation. In the second scenario, God's grace alone is operative in a person's salvation. Each person is on his or her own before God.

While the first is not an accurate description of how Jews understand Judaism, it does fit how Luther saw the Catholicism of his day, which he then projected back on to the Judaism of Paul's day. We in turn have been conditioned to read that as Paul's own perspective. The point is that we are so accustomed to seeing Paul refracted by Luther's fights with the church, that it's difficult to see and hear Paul on his own terms.[26]

How do we hear Paul's own voice more clearly? Here are a few things that can help us. First, remember that Paul is the Apostle to the Gentiles. His letters are directed to the Gentiles or non-Jewish followers of Jesus. He's not writing to Jews. Yes, he speaks about Jews in his letters, but he's writing primarily to Gentiles. Mark Nanos suggests the phrase "for non-Jews in Christ" should be added to the beginning of many sentences in Romans.[27] Try reading Paul that way and see how that changes things.

Second, Paul is one smart cookie, and a master rhetorician. Sometimes he uses Pharisaic forms of biblical interpretation, presumably learned from Rabban Gamaliel, a deeply respected teacher of the Torah.[28] At other times he's making use of a rhetorical style called diatribe. That's the case in Romans. More theater than epistle, diatribe is written for several voices including regular changes from the singular to the plural as well as first-, second-, and third-person speech. It's emotionally packed, deliberately amped up to get a positive or negative response from the listeners. In some sections of Romans Paul is dialoguing with Gentile believers in Christ, in other sections with Jewish teachers. But all of it is addressed to his Gentile listeners, all for the purpose of schooling them in God's righteousness and their privileged place in it.

Set on a two-dimensional page, it's hard to recognize Romans as a diatribe. There are no stage notes about the characters or dialogue partners. Paul did not leave any footnotes or explanations scribbled in the margins. All of that he entrusted to the letter carrier, likely Phoebe, a deacon and leader in the church.[29] It's thought that she not only delivered the letter to the church at Rome but also read it and acted out the various parts.[30]

We've seen already that Paul identifies himself as a Jew. He took on and completed vows, attended synagogue, observed Jewish holidays, and reminded others that he's a Pharisee. That's an important clue about what Paul was really up to. Remember that Pharisees, unlike Sadducees, believed in resurrection. So much so that praising God for the resurrection of the dead has been preserved in a longer ancient Jewish prayer written by the rabbis, "the intellectual offspring"[31] of the Pharisees. This prayer, called the Standing Prayer (*Amidah*), is still central to the thrice daily classical Jewish prayer service and the grace after meals.

In my days in the Orthodox community, I regularly chanted it. The second of eighteen benedictions, this prayer is subtitled "powers." Nestled in there with God's other powers, resurrection—or resuscitation or restoration or revival—as it is sometimes called, is almost taken for granted.

You are eternally mighty, My Lord, the Resuscitator.[32] of the dead are You; abundantly able to save. He sustains the living with kindness, resuscitates the dead with abundant mercy, supports the fallen, heals the sick, releases the confined, and maintains His faith to those asleep in the dust. Who is like You, O Master of mighty deeds, and who is comparable to You, O King Who causes death and restores life and makes salvation sprout! And you are faithful to resuscitate the dead.

Chanted in a springy, confident tune, the blessing ends with this affirmation:

Blessed are you, *HaShem,* Who resuscitates the dead.[33]

Many modern Christians think of resurrection as the state of being in heaven one is granted after death. Each individual experiences it upon their death. But that's not what the word meant to the Pharisees of old (nor I suspect to the Jews with whom I prayed this prayer). N.T. Wright describes the Pharisaic understanding of resurrection as a two-stage process: "First, death and whatever lies immediately beyond; second, a new bodily existence in a newly remade world."[34] Resurrection, in N.T. Wright's words is "life *after* life after death."[35] There's another difference between the state of being we ascribe to heaven and this new bodily existence in a newly remade world. Resurrection isn't a solitary experience that comes to each individual as they die. Instead, because it's "life *after* life after death," after this interim period following death, everyone would be raised from the dead together to this newly remade world. Thus resurrection would be the sign that God's heavenly reign was finally being established on earth.

So when the resurrected Jesus appeared to Paul, it took him by surprise. Not that a person might actually be resurrected. But that the World to Come would begin with just one resurrection.[36] Paul took it as a sign that the prophesied End of Ages was arriving.

When we talk end times, though, don't think Revelation. It wasn't yet written. Rather think of images offered by the Hebrew prophets. Zechariah puts it this way:

And the LORD will become king over all the earth; on that day the Lord will be one and his name one.[37]

Micah, reflecting on this time, suggests that the nations (the Gentiles), will freely choose to

> go up to the mountain of the LORD,
>   to the house of the God of Jacob;
> that he may teach us his ways
>   and that we may walk in his paths.[38]

Isaiah says:

> In days to come
>   the mountain of the LORD's house
> shall be established as the highest of the mountains,
>   and shall be raised above the hills;
> all the nations shall stream to it.[39]

This end time is a glorious time in which the Jewish watchword of faith is made manifest:

> Hear, O Israel: The LORD is our God, the LORD alone.[40]

Because God is one, God's oneness will spur a remarkable unity among all the peoples on earth, as immense as the oceans themselves.[41] This is the messianic age, the kingdom of God. It speaks of a universal salvation that awaits us all in the end. This is what Paul thought was happening: the ending of one age and dawn of a new one. That meant the messianic banquet was on! All were invited—both Jews and Gentiles.

Now before you say, "But that's what I've always thought!" let me explain a bit more. Normally, we think of this invitation to the messianic banquet in context that in Christ the Law is no longer needed. So everyone becomes, essentially, Christian. But there's actually something a little different going on here.

For Paul, unity did not mean uniformity. Did you catch that? I'll say it again. For Paul, unity did not mean uniformity. In other words, Jews and Gentiles didn't need to practice faithfulness in the same way to be true to God. Yes, all peoples would adopt the righteousness of God, according to the standards set by Torah observance (remember the Jerusalem Council's decision that since Moses had been preached in all the synagogues and Gentiles were likely already following the commandments to the best of their ability, all they had to do was be sure to follow a few specific commands), but people would remain in their given state. Jews would still be Jews, Gentiles would still be Gentiles.

> Circumcision is nothing and uncircumcision is nothing; but obeying the commandments of God is everything. Let each of you remain in the condition in which you were called.[42]

Even so, Paul writes:

> There is no longer Jew or Greek, there is no longer slave or free, there is no longer male and female; for you all are one in Christ Jesus.[43]

This oneness in Christ was not achieved by letting go of Torah. Rather, Christ was the sign that Torah righteousness had come to everyone, regardless of their religious status. For Paul, it was important that the Gentiles show up for this "end of the ages" party thrown by the God of Israel as Gentiles, not as Jews. Otherwise, the messianic age with its principle of unity in diversity and universal salvation could not be fulfilled. This open invitation to the Gentiles did not spell a disrespect or a disregard for all things Jewish. Rather, since "Jews were entrusted with the oracles of God,"[44] the call was to emulate the Jewish way of life, without actually having to convert (become circumcised). In fact, if Gentiles did convert that would mean Christ had died and risen for nothing. Jesus' resurrection was the sign that the new age had come in which all people were welcomed to the banquet feast.

There was just one problem. Not all of Paul's fellow Jews read the signs of the times in the same way he did. Some flat out disagreed. Others equated unity with uniformity. If Gentiles were coming to Israel's God, the thinking went, they should convert to Judaism first. Those Gentiles who did were known as Judaizers.

Paul was deeply opposed to this. Not because there was anything wrong with Torah, Judaism, or Jewish interpretations of the Law. Just the opposite! He saw it as the ideal life of righteousness. But in this new messianic age, when the oneness of God enveloped all else, Gentiles must come as Gentiles, "freed" of the "burden" of the Law.

> Is God the God of Jews only? Is he not the God of Gentiles also? Yes, of Gentiles also, since God is one; and he will justify the circumcised on the ground of faith and the uncircumcised through that same faith. Do we then overthrow the law by this faith? By no means! On the contrary, we uphold the law.[45]

Now that God raised Christ from the dead, Paul saw his role as bringing about "the obedience of faith among all the Gentiles."[46] It was a tough job. He had to shepherd the Gentiles in such a way that they did not lose hope or lose sight of the earth-shattering significance of Christ's resurrection. And he also had to prepare the way for Jews and Gentiles—who had very different customs, ethics, values, and lifestyles—to live together.

Branches Broken and Grafted

One of my earliest introductions to evangelism went something like this: "You're Jewish? Uh-oh. If you don't believe in Jesus, you are going to hell!" Some good news, huh? Yet, Paul says of the gospel:

> It is the power of God for salvation to everyone who has faith, to the Jew first and also to the Greek.[47]

To most of us trained to read Paul the old way that still sounds like you get saved by believing that Jesus died to save you from your sins.

Quite a few years ago, I was talking with my Jewish grandmother about my Jesus experience. She leaned forward and said conspiratorially, "I just don't believe that stuff about Jesus dying for my sins." I knew what she meant. Jews have all sorts of ways to connect to God, and to reconnect when sin has intervened. Why would Jesus need to die? It seems like an unnecessary intervention. Why put a middleman between us and God? For Paul, though, the word *gospel* has a whole different connotation. Remember that Matthew, Mark, Luke, and John weren't yet written when Paul wrote his letters. For him, the gospel is that all are coming to worship the one true God—Jews who have always done so, and now Greeks. Thus,

> There is no distinction between Jew and Greek; the same Lord is Lord of all and is generous to all who call on him. For, "Everyone who calls on the name of the Lord shall be saved."[48]

Plenty of Gentiles caught the vision and believed. Less so with Jews. Well, what of Jews who did not believe? Working with the image of a wild olive tree, Paul writes that the natural branches are the Jewish people. Some of them have been broken off so that all the Gentile believers can first come in. They are grafted into this tree as an act of grace by God. But in the end, "all Israel will be saved."[49] According to this understanding of Paul, there is no replacement theology, no supersessionism. For Paul, Gentiles and Jews together make up the people of God. The inclusion of one does not mean the replacement of the other. Are you still with me? In addition, their call is not necessarily to spread faith *in* Jesus, but to help spread the faith *of* Jesus. It turns out that the Greek word can be understood either way. Just like the disciples of old, who followed Jesus closely, we are to imitate Jesus' way of doing things. Having his kind of faith is the key to the life of faithfulness. In essence, Gentiles have been grafted onto the wild olive tree to help accomplish the biblical mandate first given to the Jewish people: "You shall love the LORD your God with all your heart,...soul, and...might." And, yes, your neighbor as yourself.

Has Paul rejected the Torah? In the old way of reading Paul, yes. Reading him again for the first time, no. Rather than declaring Judaism null and void, he affirms the Jewish people, the Jewish God, the Jewish Torah, and the Jewish way of life. At the same time, he affirms the inherent value of Gentiles and their rightful place in the World to Come. Most of all he affirms that the one God is God of all peoples. And that all can be one in God.

Sadly, in the end, this is not the way Paul has been remembered or read. In Chapter 4, we saw the vitriol that downplayed and denigrated Jewish identity. But if the participants at my workshops are any indication, people just may be ready for this new understanding of the relationship between Jews and Gentiles, and the one God who unifies us, just as we are. People are hungry for a universal salvation that provides for unity in diversity and the righteousness of God above all. Personally, I am more than ready to surrender the doubt, the distance, and the dissonance I have experienced between my Jewish self and my follower-of-Jesus self. Who would've thought that Paul would be the one to help heal this division in me? May wonders never cease!

6. A New Heaven and a New Earth

Idol-Wrecking and God-Wrestling

Temple Israel in Waterbury, Connecticut, is the Reform temple my family attended during my grade school years. It's where my two older brothers had their bar mitzvahs, where I attended Purim carnivals dressed up as Queen Esther, where I ate potato latkes, applesauce, and sour cream at our religious school celebration of Chanukah, where I sneaked an extra cinnamony-sweet *rugelach* after Friday night Sabbath services, and where two very large hooked rug wall hangings caught my eye. They hung down side by side on the exposed brick wall inside the sanctuary. The first was of Abraham destroying the idols in his father's workshop. The second was of Jacob wrestling with the divine being at the river Jabbok. As we recited psalms on Friday night from the old 1956 dark blue *Union Prayer Book* and I wondered, restlessly, how many ways there were to say that God is worthy of praise, my eyes returned again and again to these images. Long before screens and digital media made powerful use of imagery in worship services, these wall hangings, like stained glass, touched me at a place deeper than words. In retrospect, I realize they imbued me with the sense of what it means to be human, what it means to be a Jew.

From Abraham smashing the idols I gained the sense that idolatry is wrong. Pretty straightforward. But even more, I learned there will be things that appear to be true but they are not. Get rid of them. Pursue truth even if it means upsetting others around you. From Jacob wrestling the divine being I gained the sense that to be a good Jew is to be a God-wrestler. Engage, wholeheartedly, with God. Ask questions and don't let go until you get answers. Even though you will bear some scars from the encounter, it will be worth the blessing. Maybe that's why I never could relate to "Trust and Obey" as a hymn of faith: "Trust and obey, for there's no other way to be happy in Jesus, but to trust and obey." Horrors! Now I'm not saying I couldn't use some of that quiet acceptance the song counsels, but it seems to me that God welcomed the interaction with Jacob. In the end didn't the man/angel/LORD acknowledge that Jacob had prevailed? In the end, didn't the divine being bless him?

I had no idea how much those images would propel me throughout life. When some family members looked askance at my interest in Orthodoxy, I responded, "I have to see for myself." That was the spirit of Abraham and Jacob. When Reb Motti urged me, "Stay here in this community; learn with me about Jesus," again, I had to say, "I have to see for myself." Again, that was the spirit of Abraham and Jacob. When it occurred to me that the Jesus who came to me was different than the Jesus being preached in the church, I figured I better see for myself what was going on. Once again, I felt the spirit of Abraham and Jacob.

I suppose it's no coincidence that Jacob and I are connected. Given to me at birth, my Hebrew name *Ya'akova,* is the feminine form of Jacob (*Ya'akov*). At the end of the nightlong tussle, Jacob's name was changed to Israel, meaning he who wrestles with the divine. Although like Jacob, my spiritual journey led to a new name and identity for me, *Ya'akova* stayed. When the shoe fits wear it.

Temple Israel has gone the way of many small congregations; it has merged with another temple and changed its name. I don't know where those wall hangings are now. But the lessons live on in me. Be an active participant in life, in faith, in your walk with God. Throw yourself into it. And don't be afraid to wreck some idols along the way or to wrestle with God. That's how the blessings will come.

This openness to life landed me first in the Orthodox community, then after a vision from Jesus where I heard the call to ministry and joined a church. I became a pastor and served churches. Later, I left local church ministry to take on a greater role in the task of building bridges of understanding. Now I stand with one foot in the church and one in the synagogue, a thoroughly Jewish follower of Jesus.

I used to look at my life as a straight line: As I grew, I figured I was moving from point A to point B to point C and onward. Hopefully upward, definitely onward. From that vantage point, however, my life made no sense. Who goes from a deep interest in science to a life of deep faith, then from Reform Judaism to Orthodox Judaism, and then leaps into Christianity, only to embrace Judaism again? It's crazy, right? But when I look at my life as a spiral, curving through new territory then coming round again to revisit prior principles, values, interests, and commitments from a new vantage point, integrating some and letting go of others, then this makes sense.

In the long arc of history, the journey of the church is like that too. We fell in love with a Jewish leader, the movement grew organically within Judaism and then over the centuries moved away from it, yet all the while holding seeds of our mother faith within our practice, belief, most sacred texts, teachings, and Teacher. At the same time, we proclaimed ourselves, sometimes violently and viciously, as "not that." The distance proved disastrous, false, bereft of the Kingdom. You can't claim victory in Jesus while standing on the neck of your elder brother. And now we are coming around again to renew relations and look at our own need for the Jewish people.

Likewise, the Jewish journey is like that. Our rich Jewish teaching and practice, from feisty patriarchs and matriarchs to kings and prophets, and our undying commitment to God and Torah ultimately gave rise to the teachings of Jesus, to Jewish believers in Jesus, to a vibrant messianic sect, and finally to a brand-new religion. As they took off in a new direction, we kept going, and defined ourselves in part, as "not that." In the process we disowned our most famous son and prophet. And all the riches that went with him. We met violence and contempt with fear, anger, and our own brand of counter-contempt.[1] Now we too are coming around, however tentatively, to explore what might be possible for us in this relationship and even to "engage an ancient brother in a new conversation" on our own terms.[2]

Christians and Jews, our paths are not linear, nor are they ultimately divergent. We are woven together in a spiral. Twin strands of DNA that make up something greater and infinitely more powerful than what each people is capable of individually. I'm not saying this is easy. Our history shows otherwise. Like Jacob, we bear real scars from the struggle. But the past doesn't need to define or limit our future. As we engage each other, we are bearing real blessings. As the ancient "us versus them" is being deconstructed, we are collaborating on understanding the rich heritage we Jews and Christians possess in common. Psychic scars are healing. Dark hurt is fading. Closed postures are opening. Healing is happening. For just as Christians can no more claim lasting victories for the kingdom of God while persecuting Jews, neither can Jews claim to shine our full light to the nations as long as we keep those very people at bay. Our histories and our destinies are deeply intertwined. Our treasures lay buried in overlapping fields.

In this process, we need to remember the feisty forebears of Jesus: Abraham and Jacob. Idol-wrecking and God-wrestling is empowering. And scary. Like Abraham, once you've wrecked the idols, there's no going back; you can only go forward to a place only God knows. The Presence of God beckons us down the road. When Jacob finished wrestling with the divine being and emerged from that long night with a new name, he limped on to reconcile with his estranged brother. He was no longer the Jacob of the past; he was a new man with a new name: Israel or God-Wrestler. Esau might have killed him—Jacob was certainly afraid of that—instead he recognized something new in his brother and accepted him. They embraced and wept. Both brothers were blessed with a new beginning.

Post-Holocaust Christianity and Judaism are at a new beginning. We have come through a long night. We have wrestled with our histories, our traditions, our choices, our mistakes. Now a new dawn is breaking. It is time to go forward. My sense is that this journey will lead us to a greater reconciliation. I imagine new collaborations, new learnings, new respect, new ways to serve each other and the God we love.

Not that it will all be easy. I imagine we will also discover new layers of fear and prejudice and more subtle forms of violence and contempt to let go of. My work in the black church has taught me about that process firsthand. When I first moved into a leadership position at Scott United Methodist Church, it caused some waves. At first, I thought they were ripples. That was due only to the politeness of the people; they were protecting me from what must have felt like storm surges. One African American seminary professor who worshiped at Scott UMC called me in to her office at the Iliff School of Theology and asked, "What are you doing at this church, really?" She wanted to make sure I understood the white privilege I carried and the delicate balances of power it threatened; it had taken African Americans a long time to get to where they were and they didn't need me messing with it. Much as I didn't see myself as white, I understood the privilege she spoke of. Applying it to my own religious experience I could only imagine how the Jewish community would have felt about a Gentile stepping into a leadership role: unsure, ill at ease, suspicious at the very least. But what drew me in to Scott UMC wasn't a desire to usurp power; it was a desire to share it. At the same time I joined Scott UMC, I was taking seriously the call I heard again and again during my coursework at Iliff: step over the lines that fear has drawn. Be open, in the spirit of Jesus, to radical love of the other.

Some people threatened to leave the church if I stayed, others actually did. Many more, including Mrs. Polk, embraced me. The African American pastor, Rev. Aaron Gray, who had invited me to be his associate pastor, stood toe-to-toe with the concerns being expressed. His courageous stand made a space for all of us to work through our differences. In the beginning, none of us would have said, out loud anyway, that we were prejudiced or racist. Or that we saw ourselves as better or worse than the other. But we all, I suspect, had hidden layers of fear, mistrust, anger, and stereotypes to come to terms with. In the end love prevailed, buoyed by prayer and many a long talk. I left, as I said before, an honored member of the family. No mistake, I suppose, that my own family name had been Scott. Another turn of the spiral.

My point is we had work to do. Excitement and engagement brought me to the church. Welcome and gracious hospitality kept me there. Even so, this would be no easy arrangement. There were idols to overturn, stereotypes to wrestle, and fears to name. None of us knew how it would turn out. It might have been a church split. Or worse. But when we gave ourselves the space to engage our hidden fears we were instead blessed.

From Monologue to Dialogue

On a grander scale, that's the kind of transformational work Christians and Jews have engaged in. Rising from absolute bottom during Hitler's Germany, made possible by the long teaching of "contempt for the Jews," the Roman Catholic Church, in consultation with the Jewish community and others, began the careful and conscientious work of reevaluating their doctrines, liturgy, teaching, and theology.[3] As a result, they dropped the charge of deicide or murder of God against Jews, began to insist on appropriate teaching about Jews and Judaism, discouraged the evangelizing of Jews, changed inflammatory anti-Jewish Holy Week liturgy, recognized the central role of the Land of Israel in God's covenant with the Jews, and acknowledged God's ongoing and unbroken covenant with the Jewish people. These were watershed changes, which later popes have built on.

Protestants followed suit. In 1991, for instance, European Lutherans distanced themselves from Luther's outrageous statements about Jews and Judaism, "On the Jews and Their Lies," and rejected "the traditional Christian 'teaching of contempt' towards Jews and Judaism."[4] In 2010, building on a 1987 statement, the Presbyterian Church USA acknowledged that it is called to examine itself "in order to avoid explicit or implicit teaching of contempt for Judaism and Jews."[5] In 1996, building on a 1972 document, United Methodists adopted "Building New Bridges in Hope," which acknowledges the Jewishness of Jesus, affirms God's unbroken covenant with Jews, repents of Christian persecution of Jews and complicity in the Holocaust, condemns anti-Semitism, and calls for working together with Jews "in anticipation of the fulfillment of God's reign."[6] Local and regional dialogue between Jews and Christians is increasingly common.

Warmed and deeply heartened by these remarkable shifts in Christian teaching, over 150 Jewish leaders, representing a variety of Jewish denominations, have responded. In 2000, they issued *Dabru Emet,* (Speak the Truth). It offered eight brief statements about how Jews and Christians may relate to one another, perhaps most importantly acknowledging the place of Christianity in God's work and calling upon Jews to respect it. The document says, "We believe it is time for Jews to learn about the efforts of Christians to honor Judaism. We believe it is time for Jews to reflect on what Judaism may now say about Christianity."[7]

We do indeed live in extraordinary times. Recovering from the ovens of Auschwitz, Christians and Jews have successfully undertaken a gargantuan effort to move from monologue to dialogue, from hurt and suspicion, to acknowledgment and respect. As if on cue, *On Heaven and Earth: Pope Francis on Faith, Family and the Church in the 21st Century,* a book co-written by Pope Francis and his Argentinian colleague and friend, Rabbi Abraham Skorka, was released in English in April 2013. After two thousand years of enmity, prejudice, and violence, this grand sweep of reconciliation from the local to the global is historical and breathtaking.

It has even created space for Muslims to enter the public arena of interfaith dialogue. In 2007, 138 Muslim clerics and scholars representing every branch of Islam sent a beautifully worded and carefully researched letter to Christian leaders. This letter, "A Common Word Between Us and You," stated that as the two largest world religions, the peace of the world depends on peace between Muslims and Christians.[8] It used as its reference point the Hebrew Bible teachings of love of God and neighbor, saying they were common to both Islam and Christianity.

Now, if we Christians and Jews are to take the next steps of fellowship, respect, and understanding building on our shared principles, we must be ready to risk still more in order that we and others may be blessed all the more. Given that Jesus was a deeply faithful Jew, that his whole life, teaching, death, and resurrection were shaped by this identity; given that the early church understood the Jewishness of Jesus and his place among the chosen people; given that Gentiles/Christians have been grafted in to God's covenant with the Jewish people to help accomplish the Jewish/biblical mandate: "You shall love the LORD your God with all your heart, and with all your soul, and with all your might" and "your neighbor as yourself" in order to be "a light unto the nations"[9]; given that the church, historical persecutions of Jews notwithstanding, has done a mighty fine job at this in ways large and small, bringing people to knowledge of the God of Israel; and given that much has been done since the Holocaust to set right what has been askew in Christian belief and behavior, isn't it time to help shape what is emerging next in this transformative time? In the idol-wrecking, God-wrestling spirit of Abraham and Jacob, I'd like to suggest three critical shifts to the church and one to the synagogue that will help us do just that.

1. Go All the Way

Church, it's time to go all the way in embracing the Jewish Jesus. Yes, Jesus is seen as a Jew in many pulpits and pews, but usually as an exception, an anomaly. In too many sermons, commentaries, and hymnals his teachings on love, inclusion, and forgiveness are set up as a contrast against the Jews and Judaism of his day. What makes him distinctive, we say, is that he's not like the other Jews. *He* reached people on the margins. *He* talked to women. He ate with sinners and tax collectors. But these characterizations of a Jewish Jesus are still distorted. Dr. Amy-Jill Levine explains why:

> Jesus becomes the rebel who, unlike every other Jew, practices social justice. He is the only one to speak with women; he is the only one who

teaches nonviolent responses to oppression; he is the only one who cares about the "poor and the marginalized" (that phrase has become a litany in some Christian circles). Judaism becomes in such discourse a negative foil: whatever Jesus stands for, Judaism isn't it; what Jesus is against, Judaism epitomizes the category." [10]

Yes, Jesus reached out to all kinds of people. Yes, he counseled mercy and patience. Yes, he healed and set people free. But rather than see Jesus as different from the Jews around him, I suggest it is time to see Jesus' ministry as a natural evolution of the whole history of Jewish teaching, ethics, morality, practice, and service of God. Otherwise he serves as an archetypal anti-Jew.

Think about it. If Jesus was fully Jewish, operating in a Jewish context, living a Jewish life, studying Jewish texts, praying to a Jewish God, clothing himself in the Jewish commandments, where else did it come from? If we believe that Jesus was one with the God of Israel, then surely, Jesus drew upon the same Source and sources that inspired all the other teachers, miracle-workers, prophets, and kings that preceded and surrounded him. Quite often the rabbis of his era were arriving at the same conclusions he was, from the Golden Rule, to teachings on Sabbath, the importance of love of God and neighbor. [11] Others were engaged in calling disciples, healing, and miracle-working. Even his interactions with women, children, and Gentiles were not anomalous. [12]

More than that, the Hebrew Bible/Old Testament is marked by theological and behavioral leaps, beginning with Abraham's innovation that God is one, not many; continuing with Moses' skilled but previously unknown leadership in leading the Israelites from slavehood to peoplehood; game-changing visions from prophets; and the courageous renewal of Judaism under Nehemiah and Ezra after the return from Babylonian exile. Jesus is the product of generations of Jewish innovators, completely in line with the spiritual genius that went before him and even those that came after him. Paul wasn't kidding when he said about his fellow Israelites, "to them belong the adoption, the glory, the covenants, the giving of the law, the worship, and the promises; to them belong the patriarchs, and from them, according to the flesh, comes the Messiah, who is over all, God blessed forever. Amen." [13]

Putting this perspective into practice will take a renewed scholarship among preachers, pray-ers, poets, professors, and Bible study writers and teachers. I realize it's going to take some work to leave behind comfortable but dishonest dichotomies and ready stereotypes. This won't be easy for already overworked church leaders. But there are many excellent resources that can help, many of which have been noted throughout this book. It's worth the effort. We are grand participants in a historic reconciliation, the fruits of which are only beginning to be realized.

Understanding that Jesus operated within a rich spiritual and theological context is essential for deconstructing three attitudes: first, lingering anti-Judaism; second, Jesus as anti-Jew; and third, subtle "us versus them" dynamics. While denominations have repented of these attitudes, the fulfillment of that work remains to be done in individual pulpits, in Bible studies, and in human hearts. The more we get our theology and teaching right, the more space it creates for healing between Jesus and his own people.

Left unchecked, these negative us versus them dynamics will continue to play out: Jesus stood against Pharisees, or Sadducees, or high priests, or scribes, or religious leaders, or the Temple, or moneychangers, or righteous people, or people who lived by the Sabbath or purity laws. Therefore, in order to stand with Jesus, I, too, must stand against someone else. That by necessity creates enemies. We have rehearsed that all the way to the Holocaust. In our rush to stand with Jesus we have set ourselves against such a wide variety of people that we Christians have isolated ourselves. Who's left to either stand with us or against us? No doubt our increasingly open society with a growing ethnic plurality will continue to identify new people who are not yet "in." In the meantime, the religion of love has become rigid and exclusionary. Could this be why church rolls are shrinking while "alumni of the church" are growing in numbers? Many preachers, already sensitive to any appearance of anti-Judaism, try to get around it by keeping the contrasts but substituting "the church" or "church leaders" or "people like us" for any of the aforementioned categories of Jewish people in the New Testament. Dialing it down this way minimizes friction, yes, but it also distances or even erases Jesus from his Jewish people.

So if Jesus' particular approach to life is grounded in the Judaism of his day, then what is distinctive about his ministry? Here's what I see. First, Jesus not only healed and restored people (often affirming purity laws and the Sabbath when he did), he did it as a sign of the kingdom of God. It was the Kingdom that made his ministry distinctive and his self-stated purpose. First he announced it, then he enacted it through miracles and healings, then God inaugurated it through his resurrection.[14] Paul, too, spoke of it often.[15] In other words, the kingdom of God was a very big deal. Yet we downplay it. This leads to my second recommendation to the church.

2. Refocus on the Kingdom of God

Is it possible to overemphasize the person of Jesus? I'm going out on a limb here. I think the answer is yes. And I think we've done it. The music of "Christian radio" reduces the message of Jesus to personal love, forgiveness, and freedom. It may make us feel good, but it's all too often separated from Jesus' own message and personal mission statement. And it's not just the ubiquitous praise music that's uber Jesus-centric. As a preacher friend once wryly commented, "The right answer to every question in church is 'Jesus'!" That makes for a situation I doubt Jesus would have approved of.

> According to the Gospels of Matthew, Mark and Luke, Jesus spoke more about the kingdom of heaven than of himself. If, however, we listen carefully to the content of the sermons preached week after week, month after month, year after year, decade after decade from our pulpits, we cannot easily escape the impression that at best we have a blurred vision of the kingdom of heaven or at worst entirely lost sight of it.[16]

Have we substituted a personal relationship with Jesus for his own personal message to us? Biblical scholar John Dominic Crossan notes, "The historical Jesus did not send others out to speak about himself or bring others to him."[17] In fact, he often silenced people who wanted to praise him for his miraculous healings. He seemed not to want to bring attention to himself.

But the message of many churches seems to be to "bring people to Christ." Never mind that Jesus warns, "Not everyone who says to me, 'Lord, Lord,' will enter the kingdom of heaven, but only one who does the will of my Father in heaven."[18] He seems less interested in belief in him than righteous action by believers. Rather than being self-focused, Crossan notes that Jesus told his followers "they could do just what he was doing. They could heal one another, share their food together, and thereby bring the Kingdom into their midst."[19] It was an empowering message.

Refocusing on the kingdom of God not only reaffirms the heart of Jesus' teaching but reconnects him with his deeply Jewish mission. Both Jews and Christians anticipate the reign of God, whether calling it the kingdom of God, the messianic age, the world to come, or the new heaven and new earth. Jews are awaiting the first coming. Christians are awaiting the second coming. I figure when the Messiah or messianic age does arrive, our differences will probably be cleared up. But what do we do in the meantime? Lounge on the sidelines? No! Both Jews and Christians are called to an active anticipation of this new heaven and new earth, this messianic age.

Reform Judaism sees itself as "partners with God in *tikkun olam*, repairing the world," to "help bring nearer the messianic age."[20] Conservative Judaism teaches "every individual human being must live as if he or she, individually, has the responsibility to bring about the messianic age."[21] Neither of these is unlike Christian teachings that see each person as the hands and feet of Christ. All of our traditions call and empower us to do good in response to God's grace. Together, we may champion social justice projects, address injustices, right gender imbalances, overcome ethnic hatreds, nourish hungry and thirsty people, clothe naked people, restore sick people, stamp out diseases, and protect and steward the earth for future generations. Even more than that, as we live into the Kingdom together, we will also study, pray, and meditate together, and draw wisdom from each other's spiritual practices. In the spirit of our shared hopes for the Kingdom, the good we can now enact is unimaginable to previous generations. Our unity in diversity frees up considerable energies to brighten a darkened world.

Church historian Diana Butler Bass notes, "the first Christians believed that Jesus would restore the kingdom; medieval Christians believed that the church was the kingdom; Reformed Christians believed that true Christians embodied the kingdom in word and sacrament; and modern Christians believed they could create the kingdom through their work. But there has also been another story about the reign of God— the notion that God's people anticipate and participate in the kingdom through spiritual practices."[22] The spiritual practices she goes on to name include prayer, hospitality, forgiveness, charity, and stewardship. These are akin to Jewish spiritual practices of worship, service to God, study, charity, and acts of loving kindness that Judaism teaches will hasten the arrival of God's reign on earth. None of us can make the kingdom of God come. But we can practice being ready for it.

Inspired in part by "A Common Word Between Us and You" and the practice of planting trees in Israel to make the desert bloom,[23] I spearheaded the planting of an Interfaith Peace Forest in 2010.[24] This forest was to be a living symbol of our ability to restore the creation, strengthen interfaith relations, and recommit ourselves to our sacred teachings about stewardship of the earth. On October 10, 2010, one hundred Jews, Christians, Muslims, and friends gathered on a rainy day in Denver to plant over one hundred trees and shrubs. Our efforts helped transform a previously industrial area near the old airport into an urban greenway along the Sand Creek. It was uplifting and inspiring. My friend John, a self-proclaimed redneck in a ball cap, worked alongside Fatuma, a young Muslim woman in *hijab* that covered her hair, to plant a very large tree that had been placed earlier in the day by Jonathan, the Jewish husband of a member of our steering committee. Each was caught off guard by the willingness of the other to interact. By the end of the day, when those who remained gathered in an impromptu circle to express gratitude and praise God, it was hard to distinguish our tears from the raindrops that fell from above. As I watched this scene unfold, I couldn't help but think it was the foretaste of another common ground we Jews and Christians share, the image of a new heaven and a new earth.

This leads me to my last suggestion. If we reconnect Jesus the Jew with the long line of spiritual innovators that define Judaism and reconnect Jesus with his primary message, again a Jewish one, then it's time to take to heart Paul's view of the proper relationship between Jews and Gentiles as laid out in Romans 11. Taking this view to heart will allow us to reimagine our ultimate salvation.

3. Seek a New Heaven and a New Earth

As I've said before, for Christians salvation is generally thought of as a state one attains when you believe in Jesus. Many equate it with heaven and life eternal with Jesus Christ. It's certainly not for people who don't make a break with the supposedly regressive, oppressive, legalistic, unenlightened Judaism Jesus stood against. In other words, from a traditional Christian perspective, it's not for Jews. You gotta believe in Jesus to get in.

There is, however, another way to look at salvation that is more biblical and more inclusive. Remember that as an apostle to the Gentiles Paul understood he was spreading the good news of the resurrection of Jesus. To him this good news meant God had inaugurated the messianic age,[25] and with it universal restoration and salvation. Not only did Paul say "all Israel will be saved" but "salvation has come to the Gentiles."[26] From Paul's perspective, that's pretty much everyone, isn't it?

> For I am about to create new heavens
>   and a new earth;
> the former things shall not be remembered
>   or come to mind.[27]
> For as the new heavens and the new earth,
>   which I will make,
> shall remain before me, says the LORD;
>   so shall your descendants and your name remain.[28]
> But, in accordance with his promise, we wait for new heavens and a
> new earth, where righteousness is at home.[29]
> Then I saw a new heaven and a new earth; for the first heaven and the
> first earth had passed away, and the sea was no more.[30]

Related to these texts is the idea that Israel's God gathers in and blesses "all nations and tongues" of the world.[31] It's not a coercive gathering. Rather different peoples "stream"[32] to the mountain of the Lord. People are free to be who they are and still worship one God. Jews come as Jews and Gentiles come as Gentiles.

Seeing Jesus and his message as fully Jewish allows us to receive the final gift of universal restoration and salvation. Gladly, it helps to put an end to exclusivistic religion and instead refocuses on the One who came for all.

> Repent therefore, and turn to God so that your sins may be wiped out, so that times of refreshing may come from the presence of the Lord, and that he may send the Messiah appointed for you, that is, Jesus, who must remain in heaven until the time of universal restoration that God announced long ago through his holy prophets.[33]

In keeping with this idea of universal salvation, I have one final suggestion for Jews, and to some extent Christians.

Accept Jewish Followers of Jesus

Jewish followers of Jesus are here to stay. Even as we follow Jesus, we still see ourselves as Jewish. My suggestion is that the Jewish community accept this. You don't have to agree with it. You don't have to like it. You don't even have to do it yourself. But it is a widespread reality.

Jews within the Messianic Jewish community represent the rich tapestry of the Jewish world and come from all branches of Judaism—including Orthodox, Conservative, Reform, Reconstructionist, Renewal—and the various Jewish subcultures of the world, such as Ashkenazi, Sephardic, Ethiopian, and Asian. Messianic Judaism is growing in Israel, and the center of the movement is slowly shifting to the Land.[34]

In fact, by engaging with Jesus and the New Testament, many of us Jewish believers have come to claim our Judaism more strongly than ever before. We too are "engaging an ancient brother in a new conversation" and arriving at conclusions that turn out to be consistent with the earliest Jewish followers of Jesus. Moreover, new scholarship reveals themes in ancient Jewish texts that were previously thought "Christian" and so off-limit to Jews. These include the idea of a suffering servant, an invisible God being made visible, and the atoning power of the righteous.[35] Messianic Jewish understandings of Paul are beginning to find support in the work of respected Jewish New Testament scholars such as Mark Nanos and Pamela Eisenbaum, while the concept of a divine Messiah is supported by the work of Daniel Boyarin, professor of Talmudic Culture.[36] At the same time, Messianic Jews are responding constructively to the critiques of the Jewish community.[37]

While there have always been Jewish believers in Jesus, the movement has grown and organized on a large scale in the years since Vatican II. Messianic Judaism has over two hundred synagogues associated with it, another three hundred in loose affiliation, and two seminaries.[38] If you're uncomfortable reading this, I understand. One of my first forays into the world of Jesus followers was attending a Messianic Jewish service some twenty-three years ago. They seemed to me to be no more than evangelical Christianity dressed up with a patina of Hebrew. Since then I have shied away from Messianic Jews. These days, the movement is maturing as it moves away from its Christian evangelical roots. It is committing itself to authentic Jewish practice and identity, Jewish institutions, and Jewish well-being. Even so, Jewish followers of Jesus hold a wide diversity of beliefs and there is still much to be worked out.

Just as the reconciliation between Jews and Christians has something of the divine in it, so I believe this is a movement of God. I have no other explanation for it. I know I certainly didn't make up the vision of Jesus that launched me on this path. It didn't originate with me. God-wrestler that I am, I fought it till it made no more sense to fight. Perhaps this is part of the "Fourth Great Awakening" that Diana Butler Bass speaks of, or the inauguration of the world to come, that Paul recognized two thousand years ago. Whatever it is, I ask that you accept that it is. Then welcome us to the table in the grand ongoing work of dialogue and reconciliation that is bearing so much fruit. Many of us trace our belief back to the time of Jesus and Second Temple Judaism. We are a living bridge between Judaism and Christianity.[39]

One hot summer day while still living in Rawlins, Wyoming, I made arrangements to meet with Rabbi Shmuley. Rabbi Shmuley, whose name is short for Shmuel, which in turn is Hebrew for Samuel, meaning "God has heard," was a Chabad rabbi who traveled around the state reaching out to isolated and unaffiliated Jews. We met in a park named for a Russian Jew who had made Rawlins his home many long years before and contributed to its well-being. It was the one bright green spot in an otherwise dusty and dry part of town. Rabbi Shmuley asked about my Jewish life; I told him about my vision of Jesus and how I was living that out. He listened carefully. "I can't make any comment on your vision—that is between you and the Almighty. But this I can say: you have a Jewish soul. That is yours. No one can take that away from you." His smile and words of affirmation meant the world to me. I had spent so many years feeling like an unwelcome outsider to my native Judaism.

One Last Thought

Idol-wrecking and God-wrestling have led me to write this book. If I've done my job here, you too have wrestled with God in these pages. You have taken a new look at things and questioned what you thought to be true. Perhaps you are even coming away with a blessing. God-wrestling didn't begin or end with Jacob. Abraham engaged with God when he argued for the saving of Sodom and Gomorrah and Sarah when she laughed at the prospect of God's promise of a child born to her in her old age. Later, Moses tried to get out of his call. Even Jesus said to God, "Let this cup pass from me." Full engagement with God is a biblical value. To that end, I believe God welcomes this historic shift by the church to acknowledge and embrace the Jewishness of Jesus, for Jews and Christians to establish life-giving relationships with one another, and for us to forge a new way forward. I believe God wants to wrestle until we come away blessed and reconciled, in spite of the scars. Something more powerful than "us versus them" awaits us; an image that can carry us into a positive future, God's future. That's the biblical vision of the kingdom of God, the new heaven and new earth in which God's good and righteous reign on earth is made complete. May it be so! Amen.

APPENDIX

Questions for Reflection and Discussion

The following questions will help you engage the content of each chapter. They will also help you grow in your understanding of Jesus as a faithful Jew. As you read each chapter, read the Scriptures that are mentioned. If possible, find some of the sources mentioned by the author and refer to them. Above all, pray for God's guidance and wisdom as you read and think about each chapter and its questions.

Chapter 1

How does seeing Jesus as a Jew affect your perspective of Christianity? How does seeing Jesus as a Jew affect your faith?

What do you think is gained by seeing Jesus as a Jew? What do you think is lost?

How might mutual Jewish/Christian understanding of one another's traditions enrich our world today?

If you are a Christian, have you visited a temple or synagogue? What was it like for you? What would it be like to imagine Jesus worshiping there?

If you are Jewish, have you visited a church? What was it like for you? Can you see elements of Christian worship that reflect Jewish practice and/or beliefs?

Chapter 2

How do you respond to the question "Was Jesus a Christian?"

How do the writer's experiences in the first two sections of this chapter inform your response about whether Jesus was a Christian or a Jew?

As you review highlights of the biblical material examined in this chapter, what strikes you in particular about Jesus' life, ministry, and teachings?

What does it mean to you that Jesus teachings are firmly rooted in Jewish teachings?

Why, do you think, are Jesus' teachings often considered to be more Christian than Jewish?

Chapter 3

Do you draw from more than one spiritual tradition to feed your soul? If so, what traditions? How do they contribute to your faith?

What stereotypes or prejudices about Jews have you heard or recognized in our culture? In the church? In yourself?

When have you experienced sermons that compare and contrast Jesus with the Jews of his day? How did you respond to this dichotomy? How does the reality that Jesus and his first followers were faithful, practicing Jews affect your views of such preaching?

What feelings or thoughts do you have about Paul as a lifelong, practicing Jew rather than as a Jew who "converted" to Christianity?

How does seeing the early church from a Jewish perspective affect the way you understand your faith?

Chapter 4

How do you respond to the information about the church's history of anti-Semitism?

What thoughts or feelings do you have about the death of Jesus being "unexpected" to those who followed him? Why, do you think, had they not expected his death?

What does the historical material about the destruction of Jerusalem and the Temple offer to you as you consider the biblical accounts of the crucifixion of Jesus?

Which of the four explanations for why Jesus died most resonates with you? Why?

How do you respond to the three approaches to the Passion narrative? What feelings or thoughts do you have about the doubts that some have about the accuracy of the accounts of Jesus' trial and death? Do the views about the timing of the trial, Jewish law, the release of Barabbas, and the view of Pilate as somewhat sympathetic to Jesus make sense to you? Why, or why not?

What hope do you see in current dialogue between Jews and Christians?

Chapter 5

How do you respond to the idea of being chosen by God? What do you think it means to be chosen?

What do you think about the speculation that anti-Semitism might be traced to a "skewed understanding of chosenness"? Why, do you think, do attitudes of racism, prejudice against others, and anti-Semitism exist?

The author asks "Has the church taken Israel's place as the chosen people?" How do you respond to this question? Do you see yourself as chosen, too?

Read Jeremiah 31:31. How does this Scripture speak to you? How do you think it spoke to those who originally heard it from Jeremiah? How does it offer hope to both Jews and Christians?

How do you respond to the author's changed understanding of Paul's writings? How does thinking about Paul as a faithful, practicing Jew affect the way you read what he says about the Law and faith?

How does the Resurrection speak to you about God's coming reign in which all people will live according to God's ways?

How does the understanding that we have been grafted into God's covenant with the Jews speak to you?

Chapter 6

Read Genesis 32:22-30. When have you felt as though you have wrestled with God? What was it like? How was God blessing you in the experience?

In the section "From Monologue to Dialogue," the author mentions several intentional efforts by Catholics, Protestants, Jews, and Muslims to change inflammatory views of one another. How do you respond to these efforts? What more do you think might be done?

How do you think individuals can improve relationships between Christians and Jews? What specific changes do you think you might make in your perceptions and in your language?

How would an emphasis on God's kingdom contribute to better respect and understanding between Jews and Christians?

Read Romans 11. How do Paul's words speak to you about God's love for Jews? For Christians? For all people? How does the Scripture inspire you? How does it challenge you?

Overall, how does understanding Jesus as a faithful, practicing Jew affect your understanding of God? Of God's relationship with all people? How does this understanding inspire growth in your faith? Your attitudes toward those of other faith traditions?

NOTES

Chapter 1

[1] Matthew 16:15-16. See also Mark 8:29; Luke 9:20.

[2] Christopher Probst, "Martin Luther and 'The Jews': A Reappraisal," *http://www.theologian.org.uk/churchhistory/lutherandthejews.html* (2005). (Accessed 5/11/2013.)

[3] "He Touched Me," words and music by William J. Gaither, 1963. *The United Methodist Hymnal* (Nashville; The United Methodist Publishing House, 1989), 367.

[4] See Chapter 4 of my book *Green Church: Reduce, Reuse, Recycle, Rejoice!* (Nashville; Abingdon Press, 2010), for more on the Sabbath.

[5] Matthew 16:13-16.

[6] Matthew 16:17-19.

[7] Jason Byassee, private communication.

[8] Dennis Linn, Sheila Fabricant Linn, Matthew Linn, *Good Goats: Healing Our Image of God* (New Jersey: Paulist Press, 1994), 7.

[9] E.J. Dionne, Jr., "Pope Speaks in Rome Synagogue, in the First Such Visit on Record, " Special to the New York Times, Published: April 14, 1986, *http://www.nytimes.com/1986/04/14/international/europe/14POPE.html*. (Accessed 5/12/2013.)

Chapter 2

[1] Matthew 5:17-20.

[2] Reform and Reconstructionist Judaism are among those who recognize as Jews children born of a Jewish father.

[3] Genesis 17:10-12a.

[4] Both baby boys and baby girls have special naming ceremonies. For boys, it's accompanied by circumcision.

[5] Luke 2:21.

[6] Luke 1:57-60.

[7] Leviticus 12:6-8.

[8] See Exodus 13:11-12a, 13b; and Numbers 18:15-16 for more information.

[9] Luke 2:32, 38.

[10] Luke 2:39.

[11] Luke 2:40.

[12] Luke 2:42. This would have been close to the *bar mitzvah* age of thirteen when a child becomes responsible for living a Jewish life. Today *bar mitzvahs* for boys and *bat mitzvahs* for girls involve chanting from the weekly Torah portion as well as a section from the prophets (*Haftarah*). At my *bat mitzvah,* I led the Sabbath service, chanted from the week's Torah and *Haftarah* portions, gave a speech, and then we had a party!

[13] Luke 2:42-52.

[14] Proverbs 22:6.

[15] Luke 2:52.

[16] Luke 4:16-30.

[17] Matthew 4:18-22.

[18] Matthew 28:19-20.

[19] David Bivin, *New Light on the Difficult Words of Jesus: Insights From His Jewish Context* (Holland, Michigan: En-Gedi Resource Center, 2007), see p. 8.

[20] Matthew 4:17; Mark 1:15. Using the term *heaven* here is a respectful Jewish way of referring to God while avoiding the unutterable name of God revealed to Moses at the burning bush (Exodus 3:14).

[21] Matthew 6:10; Luke 11:2; see also Luke 6:20. Today Jews expect this perfection of the world at the coming of the Messiah or the Messianic Age. Christians expect it when Christ returns.

[22] New Testament references to the Kingdom are extensive. See for example: Matthew 3:2; 4:17, 23; 5:3, 10, 19-20; 6:10, 33; 7:21; 8:11-12; 9:35; 10:7; 11:11-12; 12:28; 13:11, 19, 24, 31, 33, 38, 41, 43-46, 47, 52; 16:19, 28; 18:1, 3-4, 23; 19:12, 14, 23-24; 20:1, 21; 21:31, 43; 22:2; 23:13; 24:14; 25:1, 34; 26:29; Mark 1:15; 4:11, 26, 30; 9:1, 47; 10:14-15, 23-25; 11:10; 12:34; 14:25; 15:43; Luke 1:33; 4:43; 6:20; 7:28; 8:1; 9:2, 11, 27, 60, 62; 10:9, 11; 11:2, 20; 12:31-32; 13:18, 20, 28-29; 14:15; 16:16; 17:20-21; 18:16-17, 24-25, 29; 19:11; 21:31; 22:16, 18, 29-30; 23:42, 51; John 3:3, 5; 18:36; Acts 1:6; 8:12; 14:22; 19:8; 20:25; 28:23, 31; Romans 14:17; 1 Corinthians 4:20; 6:9-10; 15:24, 50; Galatians 5:21; Ephesians 5:5; Colossians 1:13; 4:11; 1 Thessalonians 2:12; 2 Thessalonians 1:5; 2 Timothy 4:1, 18; Hebrews 1:8; 12:28; James 2:5; 2 Peter 1:11; Revelation 1:6, 9; 5:10; 11:15; 12:10.

[23] Matthew 5:3, 10, 19-20; 6:33; 7:21.

[24] Luke 6:20.

[25] For example, Matthew 13; 18; 20–22; 25.

[26] Matthew 26:29.

[27] Luke 4:43.

[28] Matthew 4:23; 8:11-12; 9:35; Luke 9:11.

[29] Acts 1:3.

[30] Matthew 10:7; see also Matthew 16:19; Mark 4:11; Luke 8:1; 9:2; 22:29-30.

[31] "World History Timeline: From Prehistory to Present Day and Everything in Between," *http://everyhistory.org/9-10.html* (Accessed 5/16/13.)

[32] Matthew 22:23-33 NIV.

[33] Matthew 22:34-36.

[34] A similar question is asked in the Talmud. Rabbi Simlai begins by saying that the 613 mitzvot (commandments) were reduced to 11 by King David (Psalm 15), to six by Isaiah (Isaiah 33:15), and then to three by Micah (Micah 6:8). Isaiah further reduced them to two: "Keep judgment and righteousness" (Isaiah 56:1).Amos came and reduced them to one: "Seek me and live" (Amos: 5:4). Habbakuk proposed an alternative: "The righteous live by their faith" (Habbakuk 2:4). The story is also told in the Talmud of Rabbi Hillel's famous reply to the Gentile who demanded he teach all of Torah while standing on one foot: "What is hateful to you, do not do unto others. That is the whole of Torah. The rest is commentary. Now go and study it."

[35] Mathew 22:37-40. Law (*Torah*) and Prophets (*Nevi'im*) are two of the three sections that make up the Ta-Na-Kh. The third is the Writings (*Ketuvim*) such as Esther, Ruth, and Psalms.

36 Luke 8:43-48; Matthew 9:20-22.

37 *The Jewish Annotated New Testament* (Amy-Jill Levine and Marc Zvi Brettler, eds.; New York: Oxford University Press, 2011) sheds bright light on many misconceptions of the status of women and the role of purity in Jesus' time. Run, don't walk, to get your copy of the volume. See especially pages 501–504.

38 Amy Jill-Levine, *The Misunderstood Jew* (New York: HarperCollins, 2006), 24.

Chapter 3

1 John 3:1-10.

2 Luke 13: 31.

3 Matthew 22:34.

4 Luke 7:36ff; 11:37ff; 14:1ff.

5 Acts 5:34-39.

6 *Introduction to Messianic Judaism: Its Ecclesial Context and Biblical Foundations* David Rudolph and Joel Willitts, gen. eds. (Grand Rapids, MI: Zondervan, 2013), 24; *The Ways That Never Parted: Jews and Christians in Late Antiquity and the Early Middle Ages* Adam H. Becker and Annette Yoshio Reed, eds. (Minneapolis: Fortress Press, 2007), 2–3.

7 Matthew 4:19.

8 This, despite the negative references to Galilee (John 1:46, 7:41, 52).

9 Matthew 4:23; 9:35; Mark 1:39; Luke 4: 14-15.

10 Luke 5:17; 7:36-50; 13:31; 14:1-14.

[11] Shmuel Safrai, "The Jewish Cultural Nature of Galilee in the First Century," *http://www.jerusalemperspective.com/4452/* (first published May 25, 2010). (Accessed 5/14/13.)

[12] John 1:40.

[13] John 3:2.

[14] Acts 15:5.

[15] See Matthew 23.

[16] Matthew 5:20.

[17] Matthew 23:2-3 NIV 1984.

[18] Amy-Jill Levine and Marc Zvi Brettler, eds., *The Jewish Annotated New Testament,* (New York: Oxford University Press, 2011), 64.

[19] "Pharisees," *The Jewish Encyclopedia, http://www.jewishencyclopedia.com/articles/12087-pharisees*. (Accessed 3/29/2013.)

[20] I think Jesus' Pharisaical fence-making can be traced to his focus on the kingdom of God. If the perfect will of God was to be done on earth that meant behavior mattered greatly. His disciples would have to take it up a notch so they could truly live the Torah: "Be perfect, therefore, as your heavenly Father is perfect" (Matthew 5:48).

[21] Matthew 5:21-24.

[22] Matthew 5:27-30.

[23] "Jewish Sects," *NIV Study Bible* (Grand Rapids, MI: Zondervan, 1995), 1473.

[24] *The Jewish Annotated New Testament,* 18.

[25] Acts 1:14.

[26] Luke 8:1-3.

[27] Women in the Gospels owned property, traveled freely, had access to their own funds, and the authority to use them. They supported Jesus in his ministry and at the time of his death. Their inclusion in this group of Jewish Jesus-followers underscores their importance and power in the movement, rather than any marginal status. See *The Jewish Annotated New Testament*, 502, for more information.

[28] Acts 1:14.

[29] Acts 2:1-5.

[30] Acts 2:6-11.

[31] Acts 2:14-36.

[32] *Baptism* comes from the Greek word meaning "immersion." Ritual immersion in flowing water was and is a common traditional practice in Jewish communities.

[33] Acts 2:47b.

[34] Acts 2:46-47.

[35] Acts 3:6, 8.

[36] See Isaiah 35.

[37] "The God of Abraham, the God of Isaac, and the God of Jacob" is a common Jewish formula used in prayer.

[38] Acts 3:1–4:4.

[39] Acts 5:14.

[40] Acts 6:7.

[41] Acts 21:20. David H. Stern points out that the Greek word translated "thousands" is *muriades,* a word that literally means tens of thousands. While there are other separate, distinct terms in both Hebrew and Greek that denote *thousand* and *thousands,* it must be noted that *muriades* was the word specifically chosen to be used here. *Jewish New Testament Commentary* (Clarksville MD: Jewish New Testament Publications, 1992), 300.

[42] Acts 28:17-24.

[43] Dagobert D. Runes, *The War Against the Jew* (New York: Philosophical Library, 1968), 122.

[44] Acts 8:1b-3.

[45] Acts 9:1-9.

[46] Acts 22:3. Gamaliel was a famous Torah teacher, a sage still known to Jews today.

[47] Acts 23:6.

[48] Romans 11:1b.

[49] For example, Acts 17:1-17.

[50] 2 Corinthians 11:22; Philippians 3:5-6.

[51] Acts 21:21.

[52] Numbers 6:1-21.

[53] Acts 21:24.

[54] Acts 21:26.

[55] Acts 18:18.

[56] Acts 16:1-3.

[57] Acts 20:16; 1 Corinthians 16:8-9.

[58] Acts 27:9. See the note for this verse in the *New Interpreter's Study Bible*.

[59] Genesis 17:10-14.

[60] Acts 15:1.

[61] Acts 15:5.

[62] Acts 15:1-35.

[63] Acts 15:17.

[64] Acts 15:19-21. "God-fearers" were non-Jews who admired Judaism and for the most part lived like Jews but who never actually converted. Perhaps the requirement for adult males to be circumcised kept them from going all the way!

[65] *New Light on the Difficult Words of Jesus,* 143. In Jewish tradition, these three tenets were later expanded into the Noahide laws, seven basic moral laws that Jewish tradition says applies to all human beings, derived from the covenant made with Noah after the Flood. They include: to establish a system of laws by which to live, to prohibit cursing God, idolatry, illicit sexuality, bloodshed, robbery, and eating flesh from a living animal.

[66] Galatians 2:6.

[67] Matthew 4:21-22.

[68] Luke 8:1-3.

[69] Matthew 10:34-36 NIV 1984; Micah 7:6.

[70] John 4:22.

Chapter 4

[1] Edward H. Flannery, *The Anguish of the Jews: Twenty-Three Centuries of Antisemitism,* Revised and updated (Mahweh, NJ: Paulist Press, 2004), 1. As quoted in Michael L. Brown, *The Real Kosher Jesus: Revealing the Mysteries of the Hidden Messiah,* (Lake Mary, FL: Front Line, Charisma Media/Charisma House Book Group, 2012), 4.

[2] For a great discussion of this topic, plus some really funny jokes, see Joseph Telushkin, *Jewish Humor: What the Best Jewish Jokes Say About the Jews* (New York: William Morrow, 1998).

[3] Matthew 27:25.

[4] Bart D. Ehrman, *From Jesus to Constantine: A History of Early Christianity, Course Guidebook* (Chantilly, VA: Transcript Book. The Teaching Company, 2004), 129–130.

[5] Ibid., 130.

[6] St. John Chrysostom, quoted in Michael L. Brown, *Our Hands Are Stained With Blood,* (Shippensburg, PA: Destiny Image Publishers, 1992), 10.

[7] Clark M. Williamson, *Has God Rejected His People? Anti-Judaism in the Christian Church* (Nashville: Abingdon Press, 1982), 110.

[8] Paul Johnson, *The History of the Jews* (New York: Harper & Row, 1987) 165.

[9] Williamson, 108–109.

[10] Joseph Telushkin, *Jewish Literacy,* Rev. Ed. (New York: HarperCollins, 2001), 187.

[11] Ibid., 194.

[12] Ibid., 197.

[13] Ibid., 192–193.

[14] Williamson, 109.

[15] Ibid., 110.

[16] Martin Luther, "On the Jews and Their Lies," Jewish Virtual Library, *http://www.jewishvirtuallibrary.org/jsource/anti-semitism/Luther_on_ Jews.html*. (Accessed 3/31/13.)

[17] Christopher Probst, "Martin Luther and 'The Jews': A Reappraisal." *http://www.theologian.org.uk/churchhistory/lutherandthejews.html* (2005). (Accessed 5/16/13.)

[18] Raul Hillberg, The Destruction of the European Jews (New York: Holmes & Meier, 1985), 7f.; quoted in Our Hands Are Stained with Blood, 8.

[19] "ADL Survey in Ten European Countries Finds Anti-Semitism at Disturbingly High Levels," *http://www.adl.org/press-center/press -releases/anti-semitism-international/adl-survey-in-ten-european -countries-find-anti-semitism.html*. (Accessed 3/31/13.)

[20] *Jewish Spirituality: A Brief Introduction for Christians* (Quality Paperback Edition, 2008), 14; quoted in Beatrice Bruteau, ed., *Jesus Through Jewish Eyes: Rabbis and Scholars Engage an Ancient Brother in a New Conversation* (Maryknoll, NY: Orbis Books, 2005), 120.

[21] Collin Hansen, "Why Some Jews Fear the Passion," *http://www. christianitytoday.com/ch/news/2004/feb20.html* (Feb. 2004). (Accessed 5/16/13.)

[22] Rabbi David Fox Sandmel, "Mel Gibson's *The Passion of the Christ*: A Jewish View," *https://www.bc.edu/content/dam/files/ research_sites/cjl/texts/cjrelations/resources/reviews/Chicago_ passion_reviews.htm* (January 2004). (Accessed 5/16/13.)

[23] In recent decades, the Passion Play has been significantly "cleaned up" so that it doesn't stir up hatred of Jews as it once did. Even so, uh . . . no, thanks.

[24] Matthew 16:22.

[25] John Dominic Crossan, *Who Killed Jesus: Exposing the Roots of Anti-Semitism in the Gospel Story of the Death of Jesus,* (HarperSanFrancisco, 1995) 12.

[26] Telushkin, 130, 138.

[27] See introductions to Matthew, Mark, Luke, and John in T*he New Interpreter's Study Bible, Rev. Ed. (Nashville: Abingdon Press, 2003).*

[28] David Noel Freedman, Editor, *Eerdmans Dictionary of the Bible* (Grand Rapids MI: Eerdmans Publishing Company, 2000) 1282–1283.

[29] John 12:27-28.

[30] John 18:11.

[31] John 19:30.

[32] Matthew 16:24; Mark 8:34; Luke 9:23.

[33] Mark 8:33.

[34] Luke 22:42. See also, Matthew 26:39; Mark 14:36; John 18:11.

[35] John 18:10-11.

[36] John 19:8-11.

[37] Telushkin, *Jewish Literacy,* 120.

[38] Mark 15:15-25.

[39] Mark 15:26.

[40] The Jewish historian Josephus and others report that riots at Passover were regularly put down. "Passover," G. J. Goldberg, *http://www.josephus.org/Passover.htm#archelaus.* (Accessed 3/31/13.)

[41] Doug Linder, "The Trial of Jesus: An Account," *http://law2. umkc.edu/faculty/projects/ftrials/jesus/jesusaccount.html* (2002). (Accessed 5/16/13.)

[42] John 11:47-48.

[43] John 11:49-50.

[44] John 11:51-52.

[45] John 11:53.

[46] John 18:38.

[47] Mark 14:53.

[48] Mark 14:56-61.

[49] See Deuteronomy 19:15.

[50] Exodus 20:16.

[51] Bruce Corley, "Trial of Jesus," in Joel B. Green, Scot McKnight, I. Howard Marshall, eds., *Dictionary of Jesus and the Gospels* (Downers Grove: InterVarsity Press, 1992), 841–851.

[52] Mark 15:6-15.

[53] Couchard, R. Stahl, "Jesus Barabbas," *http://www.radikalkritik.de/ Bar_Engl.pdf* (1930), 139. (Accessed 2/15/13.)

[54] Amy-Jill Levine and Marc Zvi Brettler, eds., The Jewish Annotated New Testament (New York: Oxford University Press, 2011), 92.

[55] Alfred Loisy, quoted in Couchard, Stahl, 146.

[56] Telushkin, *Jewish Literacy,* 123.

[57] The Jewish Annotated New Testament, 93.

[58] Telushkin, *Jewish Literacy,* 123.

[59] Beatrice Bruteau, *Jesus Through Jewish Eyes: Rabbis and Scholars Engage an Ancient Brother in a New Conversation* (Maryknoll: Orbis Books, 2005).

Chapter 5

[1] SatireWire.com, *http://www.satirewire.com/news/march02/chosen.shtml.* (Accessed 1/19/13.)

[2] "Augustine on Salvation and the Christian Life," Christian Theologians and Their Theology, *http://www.theologian-theology.com/theologians/augustine/.* (Accessed 6/10/13.)

[3] Deuteronomy 7:7-8.

[4] Midrash Bereishit 38:13; found on Visual Midrash, "Testing Abraham," by Jo Milgrom and Yoel Duman, *http://www.tali-virtualmidrash.org.il/Articleeng.aspx?art=19#language.* (Accessed 6/10/13.)

[5] Genesis 12:2-3.

[6] Genesis 15:5.

[7] Genesis 17:3.

[8] Genesis 17:8.

[9] Genesis 17:7-8.

[10] See Exodus 6:7; Leviticus 26:12; Jeremiah 30:22.

[11] *The Gates of Prayer: The New Union Prayer Book: Weekdays, Sabbaths, and Festivals Services and Prayers for Synagogue and Home* (New York: Central Conference of American Rabbis, 1975) 704.

[12] Mordecai Kaplan, the founder of the Reconstructionist Jewish movement dropped the concept of choseness when he let go of the idea of a personal God. See Robert M. Seltzer, "Mordecai Kaplan: Founder of Reconstructionist Judaism," *http://www.myjewishlearning.com/history/ Modern_History/1914-1948/American_Jewry_Between_the_Wars/ Reconstructionist_Judaism/Mordechai_Kaplan.shtml.* (Accessed 5/21/13.)

[13] See Matthew 26:28; Mark 14:24; Luke 22:20; 1 Corinthians 11:25.

[14] Hebrews 8:13.

[15] Jeremiah 31:31-34.

[16] Amy-Jill Levine and Marc Zvi Brettler, eds., *The Jewish Annotated New Testament* (New York: Oxford University Press, 2011), 416.

[17] Ibid., 406.

[18] Romans 11:29.

[19] *Nostra Aetate, Pope Paul VI, http://www.vatican.va/archive/hist_ councils/ii_vatican_council/documents/vat-ii_decl_19651028_nostra -aetate_en.html.* (Accessed 12/ 9/12.)

[20] Romans 7:12, 14a.

[21] Galatians 3:13.

[22] Romans 7:6.

[23] Romans 3:2; 9:6.

[24] For more on this, see "Introduction to Romans" and "Paul and Judaism," by Mark Nanos, in *The Jewish Annotated New Testament,* and Pamela Eisenbaum, *Paul Was Not a Christian: The Original Message of a Misunderstood Apostle* (New York: HarperOne, 2009). See also *Surprised by Hope: Rethinking Heaven, the Resurrection, and the Mission of the Church,* by N.T. Wright (New York: HarperOne, 2008).

[25] For those who may be aware of the New Pauline Perspective (NPP), Eisenbaum's and Nanos's work is even more cutting edge than that! N.T. Wright's work is considered part of the NPP. See for example, N.T. Wright, *Surprised by Hope: Rethinking Heaven, the Resurrection, and the Mission of the Church* (New York: HarperOne, 2008).

[26] Pamela Eisenbaum, *Paul Was Not a Christian: The Original Message of a Misunderstood Apostle* (New York: HarperOne, 2009), 48–54, 88–91.

[27] Lecture: "Paul and the Jewish Tradition," Mark Nanos, *http://www.youtube.com/watch?v=5cpJbMsy9MQ,* at 39:02. (Accessed 5/22/13.)

[28] Acts 5:34; 22:3.

[29] Romans 16:1-2.

[30] *The Jewish Annotated New Testament,* 257.

[31] "Olam Ha-Ba: The Afterlife," *http://www.jewfaq.org/olamhaba.htm.* (Accessed 5/24/13.)

[32] Variously translated resuscitates, resurrects, revives, and restores.

[33] Rabbi Nosson Sherman, ed., *The Complete Artscroll Siddur: Weekday/Sabbath/Festival* (New York: Mesorah Publications, 1984), 101. Also, *HaShem* meaning "The Name" is a respectful Jewish way of referring to God without uttering the unutterable Hebrew name of God.

[34] N. T. Wright, Surprised by *Hope: Rethinking Heaven, the Resurrection, and the Mission of the Church* (New York: HarperOne, 2008), 41.

[35] Ibid., 151.

[36] Known variously as the World to Come, the Reign of God, the kingdom of God, the End of the Age, the new age, or the messianic age.

[37] Zechariah 14:9.

38 Micah 4:2.

39 Isaiah 2:2.

40 Deuteronomy 6:4.

41 Habakkuk 2:14.

42 1 Corinthians 7:19-20.

43 Galatians 3:28.

44 Romans 3:2.

45 Romans 3:29-31.

46 Romans 1:5.

47 Romans 1:16.

48 Romans 10:12-13.

49 Romans 11:26.

Chapter 6

1 Much later I have come to find out that the Talmudic references to Jesus are not flattering. See *Jesus in the Talmud,* by Peter Schafer (Princeton, NJ: Princeton University Press, 2007).

2 See for example *Jesus Through Jewish Eyes: Rabbis and Scholars Engage an Ancient Brother in a New Conversation,* Beatrice Bruteau, ed. (Maryknoll, NY: Orbis Books, 2001). See also *Christianity in Jewish Terms,* Tikva Frymer-Kensky, David Novak, Peter Ochs, David Fox Sandmel, and Michael A. Signer, eds. (Boulder, CO: Westview Press, 2000).

3 Beginning with *Nostra Aetate* (English) continuing on through Pope John Paul II and Pope Benedict XVI.

[4] This is the Driebergen Declaration, issued by the European Lutheran Commission on the Church and the Jewish People, representing a broad base of European Lutherans. *http://www.jcrelations.net/A_ Response_to__i_Dabru_Emet__i.1673.0.html.* (Accessed 3/1/13.)

[5] "Christians and Jews: People of God," *http://www.ccjr.us/dialogika -resources/documents-and-statements/protestant-churches/na/ presbyterian/801-pcusa10feb25.* (Accessed 5/24/13.)

[6] "Building New Bridges of Hope," T*he Book of Resolutions of The United Methodist Church, 2008* (Nashville: The United Methodist Publishing House, 2008), 308.

[7] *Dabru Emet, http://www.jcrelations.net/Dabru_Emet_-_A_Jewish_ Statement_on_Christians_and_Christianity.2395.0.html.* (Accessed 2/12/13.)

[8] "A Common Word Between Us and You," *http://www.acommonword. com/.* (Accessed 5/24/13.)

[9] Deuteronomy 6:4; Leviticus 19:18; Isaiah 49:6.

[10] *The Misunderstood Jew: The Church and the Scandal of the Jewish Jesus,* Amy-Jill Levine (NY: Harper Collins, 2006), 19.

[11] See for example, *Hillel and Jesus: Comparisons of Two Major Religious Leaders,* James H. Charlesworth, Loren L. Johns, eds. (Minneapolis: Fortress Press, 2011).

[12] See "Bearing False Witness: Common Errors Made About Early Judaism," *The Jewish Annotated New Testament,* Amy-Jill Levine and Marc Zvi Brettler, eds. (NY: Oxford University Press, 1997), 501–504.

[13] Romans 9:4-5.

[14] According to the new Pauline perspective, Mark Nanos, and others.

[15] Acts 14:21-22; 19:8; 20:24-25; 28:23, 30-31.

[16] "Toward an Unclouded Vision of His Kingdom" by Joseph Frankovich, *http://www.jerusalemperspective.com/4657/.* (Accessed 6/2/13.)

[17] John Dominic Crossan, *Who Killed Jesus? Exposing the Roots of Anti-Semitism in the Gospel Story of the Death of Jesus* (San Francisco: HarperSanFrancisco, 1996), 209.

[18] Matthew 7:21.

[19] Crossan, 209.

[20] *http://urj.org/socialaction/judaism/advocacy/.* (Accessed 2/27/13.)

[21] *Emet ve'Emunah: Statement of Principles of Conservative Judaism* (United Synagogue Book Service, 1990), 27. http://www.icsresources. org/content/primarysourcedocs/ConservativeJudaismPrinciples.pdf. (Accessed 2/27/13.)

[22] *Christianity after Religion: The End of Church and the Birth of a New Spiritual Awakening,* Diana Butler Bass (NY: HarperOne, 2012), 158–159.

[23] Isaiah 35:1-2.

[24] See also "Chapter 6: Rejoice!" in my book Green *Church: Reduce, Reuse, Recycle, Rejoice!* (Nashville: Abingdon Press, 2010).

[25] Mark Nanos, "Paul and Judaism," in *The Jewish Annotated New Testament,* 551–554.

[26] Romans 11:26; 11:11.

[27] Isaiah 65:17.

[28] Isaiah 66:22.

[29] 2 Peter 3:13.

[30] Revelation 21:1.

[31] Isaiah 66:18.

[32] Isaiah 2:2.

[33] Acts 3:19-21.

[34] *Introduction to Messianic Judaism: Its Ecclesial Context and Biblical Foundations,* David Rudolph and Joel Willits, eds. (Grand Rapids: Zondervan, 2013), 35.

[35] Michael L. Brown, *The Real Kosher Jesus: Revealing the Mysteries of the Hidden Messiah* (Lake Mary, FL: Front Line, 2012), 125–182.

[36] Pamela Eisenbaum writes in her review of *They Don't Make Jews Like Jesus Anymore* (Moment Magazine, March 5, 2012): "Boyarin argues strongly...The concept of the divine Messiah was not a deviation or even an innovation, he says. It was a prominent and long-standing Jewish idea that preceded the crucifixion of Jesus. He writes, 'While by now almost everyone, Christian and non-Christian, is happy enough to refer to Jesus, the human, as a Jew, I want to go a step beyond that. I wish us to see that Christ too—the divine Messiah—is a Jew. Christology, or the early ideas about Christ, is also a Jewish discourse, and not—until much later—an anti-Jewish discourse at all.' " *http://www.momentmag.com/book-review-they-dont-make-jews -like-jesus-anymore/. (*Accessed 5/27/13).

[37] "Reflections on Michael Wyschogrod's Critique of Jewish Christianity," Jon Olson in *Kesher, A Journal of Messianic Judaism, http://www.kesherjournal.com/Issue-18/Reflections-On-Michael -Wyschogrod-s-Critique-Of-Jewish-Christianity.* (Accessed 5/26/13.)

[38] *Introduction to Messianic Judaism: Its Ecclesial Context and Biblical Foundations* (Grand Rapids, Michigan: Zondervan, 2013) 31, 117.

[39] Ibid., 14.